Benchmarking
for Nonprofits

How to Measure, Manage,
and Improve Performance

by **Jason Saul**

FIELDSTONE
ALLIANCE

SAINT PAUL
MINNESOTA

We thank The David and Lucile Packard Foundation
for support of this publication.

Turner Publishing Company
445 Park Avenue, 9th Floor
New York, NY 10022
Phone: (212)710-4338 Fax: (212)710-4339
200 4th Avenue North, Suite 950
Nashville, TN 37219
Phone: (615)255-2665 Fax: (615)255-5081
www.turnerpublishing.com

Fieldstone Alliance is committed to strengthening the performance of the nonprofit sector. Through the synergy of its consulting, training, publishing, and research and demonstration projects, Fieldstone Alliance provides solutions to issues facing nonprofits, funders, and the communities they serve. Fieldstone Alliance was formerly Wilder Publishing and Wilder Consulting departments of the Amherst H. Wilder Foundation. If you would like more information about Fieldstone Alliance and our services, please contact us at 651-556-4500.

We hope you find this book useful! For information about other Fieldstone Alliance publications, please see the list at the end of the book or contact:

Fieldstone Alliance Publishing Center
800-274-6024
www.FieldstoneAlliance.org

Edited by Vincent Hyman
Text designed by Kirsten Nielsen
Cover designed by Rebecca Andrews

Manufactured in the United States of America

Third printing, July 2008

Library of Congress Cataloging-in-Publication Data

Saul, Jason, 1969-
  Benchmarking for nonprofits : how to measure, manage, and improve performance / by Jason Saul.-- 1st ed.
      p. cm.
  Includes bibliographical references and index.
  ISBN-13: 978-0-940069-43-5 (pbk.)
  ISBN-10: 0-940069-43-1 (pbk.)
  1. Benchmarking (Management) 2. Nonprofit organizations. I. Title.

HD62.15.S28 2004
658.4'013--dc22
                                    2004019501

Author's Note

This book is dedicated to Richard and Yolanda Saul who taught me that anything is possible—even benchmarking social change work.

Thanks to the folks at Fieldstone Alliance—Vince Hyman and Kirsten Nielsen—for their patience, hard work, and vision in making this book possible.

A special thanks to Jim Williams, Pat Jones, Donna Davidson, and the Easter Seals Benchmarking Team for their support and work.

I would also like to thank the following individuals for their thoughtful critiques of the book's first draft:

Emil Angelica
Marion Conway
Kassie Davis
Claudia Dengler
Kristin Drangstveit
Kathleen Enright
Devin Griffin
Susan Herr
Linda Hoskins

Irv Katz
Mark Kramer
Susan Lloyd
Carol Lukas
Steven McCullough
Ricardo Millett
Frank Polkowski
Sarah Solotaroff
Peter Tavernise

About the Author

JASON SAUL is a leading expert in measuring performance in the social sector. He has advised some of the world's leading nonprofits, including Boys and Girls Clubs of America, Easter Seals, American Red Cross, the Humane Society of the United States, and the Smithsonian Institution. Saul is the founder and president of Mission Measurement LLC, a firm that provides strategy and measurement services to corporations, foundations, and nonprofits. In 1994, Saul cofounded the Center for What Works, a nonprofit organization focused on benchmarking. Saul began his career as an attorney, most recently at Mayer Brown LLP in Chicago where he represented government and nonprofit clients in public finance transactions.

Saul teaches performance measurement at the Center for Nonprofit Management at Northwestern University's Kellogg School of Management. He holds a JD from the University of Virginia School of Law, an MPP from Harvard University's John F. Kennedy School of Government, and a BA in Government and French Literature from Cornell University. In 1989, Saul was awarded the Harry S. Truman Scholarship for leadership and public service. In 2001 Saul was selected as a Leadership Greater Chicago fellow.

Contents

Introduction

Now more than ever, nonprofits are focusing on results, reducing costs, squeezing more out of every dollar, and innovating on a daily basis. The key to success in today's nonprofit sector depends not just on the ability to raise money, but on the ability to demonstrate effectiveness—and improve it.

This book teaches nonprofit managers how to measure, manage, and improve their results. It details a performance-driven approach—benchmarking—that has for years been a hallmark of the business world, but is now *de rigueur* in many of America's most innovative and well-managed nonprofit organizations. Indeed, on a consistent basis, today's leading organizations seek out the best new ideas from business, top-performing peers, or competitors and, well, copy them.

> Benchmarking holds tremendous potential for the nonprofit sector. It can help an organization stimulate innovation, increase impact, decrease costs, inspire staff, impress funders, engage boards, and focus the mission.

KaBOOM!, a nonprofit that builds playgrounds in inner cities, did it by studying how businesses built easy-to-maintain web sites and used the same method to decrease its web development costs.

The *Social Security Administration* did it by improving its 800-number customer service after studying American Express, Saturn, AT&T, and the GE Answer Center.

The *Chicago Arts Partnership in Education* did it by identifying the highest margin on last year's consulting contracts and then using that baseline to raise the margin for all future contracts.

This process of measuring an organization's business processes against leaders in any industry to gain insights to improve performance is called *benchmarking*.

Benchmarking empowers any organization to make today's state-of-the-art tomorrow's industry standard.

Benchmarking holds tremendous potential for the nonprofit sector. It can help an organization stimulate innovation, increase impact, decrease costs, inspire staff, impress funders, engage boards, and focus the mission. In point of fact, most nonprofits are already benchmarking, albeit informally, through conferences, technical assistance programs, newsletters, seminars, and consultants. Now, more formal benchmarking offers nonprofit organizations a systematic and reliable tool to manage and improve performance by studying the best solutions to common problems.

So Why Bother?

Resources are tight. Time is even tighter. And who needs another task to do when there's barely even time to breathe? This is especially true for smaller nonprofits without the luxury of resources or staff. So why bother?

If you're asking these questions, you are the perfect benchmarking candidate. A critical thinker asks, Why? Benchmarking is a tool that critical thinkers use to answer that question. Why do we do things the way we do? How do others do it differently? Why should we change?

Here are three compelling reasons why you should commit your scarce resources to learning how to benchmark.

1. *You're probably already doing it.* Most nonprofit organizations, even the little guys, have a strategic plan. According to Independent Sector, 59 percent of nonprofits and 39 percent of religious congregations develop strategic plans.[1] Why—for what purpose? Ostensibly, you develop a strategic plan to help your organization set goals and determine the strategies for achieving them. Then what? How do you know if you are successful? What progress are you making? Are your strategies the best ones for accomplishing your goals? Benchmarking is designed to help you answer these questions. So many organizations go through the trouble of developing a strategic plan, but then have no way to apply it. Benchmarking brings your strategic plan to life and makes the time you spent developing it worthwhile.

2. *Control your own destiny.* Like it or not, people judge your performance each and every day. Your constituents decide whether they like your services. Your funders determine whether you used their grant dollars successfully. Donors judge whether you are worthy of their support. And your board evaluates how well you are accomplishing the mission. Each of these stakeholders is so

---

[1] Susan Wiener, Arthur Kirskh, and Michael McCormack, *Balancing the Scales: Measuring the Roles and Contributions of Nonprofit Organizations and Religious Congregations* (Washington, DC: Independent Sector, 2002).

essential to your work, but all too often, organizations feel helpless to influence their opinions. Why? Because often nonprofit managers lack the tools to set the criteria for success: 61 percent of nonprofits use outside parties to evaluate their activities, and 38 percent of religious congregations use outside evaluation.[2] Benchmarking puts you in the driver's seat and enables you to measure the success of your work, and improve it, without relying on third parties.

3. *If you don't, you may not survive.* Today, there are over 900,000 active charities in the United States.[3] And the number of nonprofits is growing faster than the gross domestic product. In 2001 alone, 81,000 organizations applied for tax-exempt status out of which 65,000 were granted. At the same time, there are only one thousand different types of nonprofit programs, according to the National Center for Charitable Statistics.[4] This means for every type of nonprofit program, there are on average 900 organizations trying to do the same thing! Odds are, someone, somewhere, some way, somehow has done what you're trying to do, better, faster, and less expensively with more creativity, better reach, and greater impact. If you don't know who this is, your supporters might just find out before you do. To compete for funding in today's environment, organizations must be able to demonstrate their effectiveness. Benchmarking helps you convince stakeholders that you are the best at what you do.

Who This Book Is For

This book is designed for those who have a stake in improving your organization's performance. This includes board members, the executive director, development staff, program staff, and volunteers. By helping you to measure and improve your organization's performance, benchmarking can be applied to all aspects of your work: financial management (through results-based budgeting and better resource allocation), strategic planning (through better mission alignment and performance management), human resources (through better morale and performance reviews), governance (through increased accountability and board engagement), fundraising (through performance reports and competitive positioning), knowledge management (through sharing best practices), and program performance (through impact analysis and better programs).

This book applies to all sizes and types of nonprofit and public-purpose organizations. Whether you're an environmental group, an advocacy organization, a cultural institution, a faith-based initiative, a community development effort, a human services organization, or a governmental entity, if you're trying to solve public problems, benchmarking can work for you.

---

[2] Ibid.

[3] According to Internal Revenue Service data.

[4] According to the Urban Institute–NCCS Nonprofit Program Classification System (www.nccs.urban.org).

A special note for small nonprofit organizations

Often, small organizations—those with budgets under $500,000 and few if any full-time staff—are reluctant to engage in benchmarking. Some feel it's too complex, time-intensive, and costly for their organizations. Fact is, benchmarking is actually most useful to the little guys—those who have no time or money to waste doing the wrong thing! Still, finding the time can be a challenge. So here are tips for how a tiny organization can benchmark at *no additional cost*.

1. Use volunteers

Dozens of organizations offer free consulting to nonprofits. Some of these—particularly those with retired business executives—are ideally suited to help nonprofits benchmark. Here are a few of the best: SCORE (Service Corps of Retired Executives) at www.score.org; ESC (Executive Service Corps) at www.escus.org, and its international counterpart, IESC (International Executive Service Corps) at www.iesc.org; the Rotary Club at www.rotary.org; and Net Impact at www.net-impact.org. Last, check out your local business and public policy schools for free interns—most have formal programs for placing students at nonprofit organizations.

2. Leverage your board

Many organizations, when asked how many people work for their organization, forget to count their board members! View your board as an extension of your organization. Benchmarking is a task ideally suited for board members who have a strong vested interest in seeing your organization improve. Ask a few to spearhead your benchmarking efforts.

3. Do it instead of a strategic plan

Benchmarking is often substituted for strategic planning. Often, organizations spend a lot of time on long-range strategic planning only to see the plan sit on the shelf. Instead, try benchmarking. It will help you set the same priorities and goals as a strategic plan, but with potentially greater precision and utility. Then benchmarking takes strategic planning one step further and helps you actually measure and improve your work.

4. Benchmark one thing that really matters

When resources are constrained, try focusing on improving just one thing. Maybe it's reducing your highest cost activity. Or maybe it's fundraising. It could even be something really straightforward like benchmarking a salary. Getting a quick win by focusing on some low-hanging fruit can demonstrate the value of benchmarking to your organization with minimal effort.

5. Collaborate with peers

Collaboration is one of the nonprofit sector's most powerful assets. If you are strapped for time, find a few of your peers and pull together a small benchmarking group. You can learn together and share responsibilities, thereby enlarging your staff's resources without cost. Also, consider working with your local management support organization (MSO), a trade association, or a larger partner to find like-minded peers. Alliance for Nonprofit Management lists over 300 MSOs: www.allianceonline.org.

6. Do it informally

This book sets out a formal process for benchmarking. But benchmarking can be done on an informal basis every day. Try to incorporate ideas in this book into your current decision-making process so that benchmarking becomes organic. When you are faced with a problem to solve, try to quantify what level of improvement you are looking for, and then ask at least one other person outside your organization how they addressed the same problem. Ask them how they measured their results. You might be surprised what you can learn in the process of resolving a problem.

7. Get a planning or capacity building grant

More and more funders are making grants available for capacity building. These grants allow you to hire consultants, bring on additional staff, and focus on improving your management to increase organizational impact. A good place to start is Grantmakers for Effective Organizations: www.geofunders.org.

How to Use This Book

This book begins with an explanation of benchmarking basics. Following that, it is organized into five chapters, each corresponding to the key steps in benchmarking. Together, these steps set forth a continuous improvement process that is designed to be used by nonprofit managers to conduct benchmarking at the organizational level, the departmental level, or the program level.

Chapter 1: Prepare Your Organization

Chapter 2: Analyze What to Improve

Chapter 3: Measure Performance

Chapter 4: Learn What Works

Chapter 5: Implement Best Practices

Using the benchmarking worksheets in this book

The worksheets found throughout this book are meant to be *used.* You can photocopy worksheets from this book or download free versions from Fieldstone Alliance's web site. Enter the following URL into your web browser to download the material:

http://www.FieldstoneAlliance.org/ worksheets

Code: W431bEN04

If you have any trouble downloading the file, you can contact the publisher at 800-274-6024. The downloadable versions are in a form that allows you to type in your responses and reformat the material to fit your benchmarking initiative. Please do not photocopy or download worksheets unless you or your organization has purchased this book.

Each step is divided into substeps that set forth discrete tasks. Worksheets help guide you to accomplish these tasks.

The best way to use this book is to start at the point most appropriate for your organization. When it comes to measuring performance and benchmarking, most organizations fall into one of three modes: the *Why* mode, the *What* mode, or the *How* mode. This book is designed to take your organization through one mode at a time; you can focus on just one mode or all three, depending on your time and preference. As you work through each mode, your organization will be building capacity and learning how to improve.

***Why* Mode** (Benchmarking Basics, Chapter 1): Organizations in this mode are trying to build the case internally for measurement. The primary issue is readiness. What is benchmarking? Why do it? Why now? What are the key drivers? How do I ready my organization to undertake this process?

***What* Mode** (Chapters 2 and 3): Organizations in this mode already know why they need to measure and improve, but they are not sure where to begin. The primary issue is focus. What kinds of things can we benchmark? What do we do first? How do we prioritize? What measures should we use?

***How* Mode** (Chapters 4 and 5): Organizations in this mode know why they are benchmarking and what they want to work on; the primary issue here is determining how to improve. How do we know what works and what doesn't? How can our organization learn and from whom? How can we apply better practices within our organization?

Bottom line: there really is no perfect time to begin benchmarking. You can jump in at any time. At any point in an organization's life cycle, benchmarking can help unify the vision, determine goals, measure performance, and improve results. The beauty of benchmarking is that it ties together the work your organization has done with strategic planning, organizational assessment, business process analysis, and performance measurement and evaluation. And it transforms these ideas into a practical tool that can help your organization improve on a daily basis—at no cost!

Benchmarking Basics

As with most things, benchmarking sprang out of necessity. Originally, the term was used by land surveyors who, while working in broad, open expanses of land, needed to mark a fixed reference point (buildings, rocks, landmarks) in order to measure distances. The business sector also came to use benchmarking out of necessity. In the mid-to-late 1970s, corporations that once dominated their particular industry came under a new and intense competition, primarily from abroad. Innovative foreign companies, primarily Japanese at the time, were selling higher quality products at the same prices it cost American companies just to manufacture them! Distraught and beleaguered, American companies knew that incremental improvements wouldn't cut it. So they searched for a way to find breakthrough improvements. What they discovered (Xerox, among the first) was a peer-learning process called benchmarking—a process that could radically transform their businesses and catapult them into a new dimension of productivity, performance, and competition.

> Benchmarking: a systematic, continuous process of measuring and comparing an organization's business processes against leaders in any industry to gain insights that will help the organization take action to improve its performance

The following are commonly used definitions of benchmarking:

> "A systematic and *continuous measurement process*; a process of continuously comparing and measuring an organization's business processes against business leaders anywhere in the world to gain information which will help the organization take action to improve its performance."
>
> —International Benchmarking Clearinghouse

"Benchmarking is the *continuous process of measuring* products, services, and practices against the toughest competitors or those companies recognized as industry leaders."

—D.T. Kearns, Xerox Corporation

"Benchmarking is the *continuous process of measuring* your current business operations and comparing them to those of best-in-class companies. Application of the knowledge gained from a benchmarking study provides a foundation for building operational plans to meet and surpass industry best practices."

—AT&T Benchmarking Group

Note that all of these definitions share the same concepts:

Continuous: Benchmarking is a constant, never-ending cycle of looking for new and better ways of doing things.

Process: Like the underlying business processes it seeks to improve, benchmarking itself is a process—a structured set of activities that seeks to bring about a desired result.

Learning: Ultimately, benchmarking is a learning process. It is a means for studying other ways of doing things, absorbing the lessons learned, and then applying that newly acquired knowledge to practice.

Measuring: Benchmarking requires comparison. In order to compare, one must have common metrics that gauge relative performance.

What Is Benchmarking for Nonprofits?

Benchmarking for nonprofits can be defined simply as a process for measuring and improving performance. Of course, multiple steps underlie this process, as this book will explain.

Benchmarking was not designed just for businesses. It was designed for organizations. Any organization (for-profit or nonprofit) with a mission and a clear set of goals can benchmark. A frequent question asked by nonprofit managers is, How can benchmarking help us if we don't have a "bottom line"? The answer is that nonprofits actually do have a bottom line, albeit a slightly different one. For-profit companies have a *profit margin*; nonprofits have a *performance margin* (see Figure 1). Impact is the nonprofit's equivalent to profit (though nonprofits can also generate income in excess of their expenses). While businesses make a profit, nonprofits make a difference. And nonprofits can measure success by gauging how much of a difference they make—how many mouths they feed, how many jobs they create, how many houses they build. If a process can be quantified and measured, it can also be benchmarked and improved.

Figure 1. Measuring Profit versus Performance

Profit margin: How much *money* did we make for the shareholders?

Performance margin: How much of a *difference* did we make for stakeholders?

Clearly, one of the primary benchmarking challenges for nonprofits is figuring out how to "quantify and measure" what they do. And while no publicly articulated, "standard" performance measures currently exist for the sector, organizations still measure every day: How many students graduate from our program? How quickly do we pay our vendors? How many people use our services? How many hits do we get on our web site? How often does our board meet? How much does it cost to raise a dollar? The key in benchmarking is not just measuring, but measuring what matters—the things that are most relevant to the success of your mission. (More about measurement in Chapter 2.)

Surprisingly, measuring success can be just as difficult for businesses. While profitability seems like an obvious measure, it isn't always the most relevant to a company's success. Take, for example, Ford Motor Company, the epitome of corporate America. Ford's mission statement says, "We are...committed to providing personal mobility for people around the world. We anticipate consumer need and deliver outstanding products and services that improve people's lives." If profitability were the only measure, Ford certainly wouldn't be realizing its mission.

What Are Best Practices?

Best practices are the products of benchmarking. They are the innovative processes (methods, policies, or programs) of other top-performing organizations that make them so successful. A best practice could be an entire program, such as a tuition-assistance program to keep inner-city kids in school, or it might be an innovative method, such as using donated software to lower technology costs. In short, a best practice is the most successful and efficient means of achieving a particular outcome for an organization.

Best practices are always relative. To determine which practices are "best" for your organization, you must first identify precisely and concretely what results your organization is trying to achieve. This is because benchmarking involves an *organic* process whereby best practices are born out of the needs and wants of a particular organization. This self-examination process is crucial to successful benchmarking; without it, you may be fishing with the wrong bait. There are now plenty of "best practice databases" available that list innovative solutions. However, divorced from the process of benchmarking, these "canned" best practices are merely orphaned ideas.

Determining what constitutes a best practice can be the most challenging part of benchmarking. What makes one practice better than another? In fact, there is rarely a "one-size-fits-all" solution to a particular problem. For example, there isn't one "best" way to run a homeless shelter or counsel a battered spouse, but there may be "better" ways. It is important to remember that benchmarking is a *comparative* approach: it helps you decide what works by comparing the performance of different processes to see which perform better than the rest. Several guiding principles can help you to identify best practices.

- Is there a proven track record of success?
- Are the results sustainable?
- Can the idea be replicated?
- Is it cost-effective?
- Does it help us achieve our mission?
- Does it fit the particular context?

What Do You Benchmark?

Basically, you can benchmark anything about your organization that you want to improve. All nonprofit organizations are made up of the same basic "DNA": processes and outcomes.

Processes are coordinated sets of activities designed to produce certain outcomes. Processes can take the form of methods, policies, or programs. Look, for example, at the processes inside a small community-based theater. For the theater,

- A *method* is a technique for performing a particular activity, such as how to track tickets sold or how to store materials from old sets
- A *policy* is a guideline governing the way a certain activity is conducted, such as requiring volunteers to sign waivers or only selling season tickets
- A *program* is an organized set of activities that delivers a service or product, such as an artist-in-residence program or a job-skills training program

Outcomes are the changes in condition or behavior that you are trying to accomplish with your processes. An outcome can be related to an internal impact (affecting staff or other people inside your organization) or an external impact (affecting constituents or others outside your organization). Nonprofit outcomes generally fall into four main impact areas: management effectiveness outcomes, financial sustainability outcomes, community engagement outcomes, and program performance outcomes. If you want to improve a particular outcome, you will need to improve the business processes inside your organization that drive that outcome. Identifying and improving those processes through adopting best practices is what benchmarking is all about.

Here are a few illustrations:

- **Benchmarking management effectiveness:** A local YMCA wants to improve the quality of its board meetings (a management outcome). To accomplish this, the organization benchmarks board recruitment, board compensation, and board participation programs (all processes) of other YMCAs, as well as other youth services organizations.

- **Benchmarking financial sustainability:** A homeless shelter wants to become less reliant on foundation grants and diversify its income streams (a financial outcome). To accomplish this, the organization benchmarks the earned-income strategies (processes) of other human services providers.

- **Benchmarking community engagement:** A political campaign wants to attract more volunteers (a community outcome). To accomplish this, the campaign benchmarks volunteer recruitment strategies (processes) of other successful campaigns across the country.

- **Benchmarking program performance:** An advocacy organization wants to improve the reach of its AIDS awareness program (a program performance outcome) so it benchmarks the results against last year's marketing effort (process) and finds that online advertising worked much better.

To determine where to start, you must first take an in-depth look at the organization to determine where improvement is most needed. This analysis requires clarity of the organization's ultimate mission, as well as the business processes (management, financial) by which the organization achieves that mission. Chapter 2 discusses how to audit your organization's performance and calibrate the measures you will use for benchmarking.

Outcomes are not just for programs

Many practitioners associate outcomes only with programs. But in fact, nonprofit performance (and ultimately mission impact) is much broader than just program results. Take the example of PipeVine, a nonprofit organization that handled online transaction processing for donations to charities. The organization's program (that is, its donation-processing services) performed well. However, PipeVine's deficient accounting and fiscal management put the organization and its customers at risk, ultimately forcing it to shut its doors. This led some observers to refer to PipeVine as the "Enron of nonprofits."* The bottom line: program performance does not tell the whole story of an organization.

* Todd Wallack, "Nonprofit Admits Spending Charities' Money: Donation Processor's Accounting Problems at Least 2 Years Old," *Chronicle of Philanthropy*, June 5, 2003, http://www.sfgate.com/cgi-bin/article.cgi?file=/chronicle/archive/2003/06/05/MN294033.DTL.

Internal versus External Benchmarking

There are generally two kinds of nonprofit benchmarking: internal benchmarking and external benchmarking. *Internal benchmarking,* or *historical benchmarking,* looks at your own organization's past performance and projects future goals based on your internal track record. Internal benchmarking asks the question, What were our results last year, and how much better do we want them to be this year? If your organization is big enough, you can also search for best practices from other chapters, affiliates, or departments. In smaller organizations, best practices are translated from one department to another. In fact, the first formal benchmarking Xerox undertook in the late 1970s was with the company's Japanese affiliate, Fuji-Xerox. Many organizations start out benchmarking internally. Internal benchmarking keeps an organization focused on its goals and generates realistic targets for employees to work toward.

External benchmarking, or *comparative benchmarking,* looks outside your organization to learn how others are meeting similar outcomes using processes that may be better, faster, or cheaper. External benchmarking asks the question, How does our organization compare to other organizations in generating a particular result? As top performers are identified, the performance of your own organization can be compared or "benchmarked" against the performances of the best in class. The lessons learned from leading organizations are then imported and translated to fit the needs of your organization. The knowledge gained through this process can exponentially increase your organization's performance, establish a proactive rather than a reactive agenda for the future, and help hone your organization's focus.

While the benchmarking methods taught in this book can be used either internally or externally, the discussion is geared more toward external benchmarking. The reasons are simple. Most nonprofits are already focused internally on solving problems, and they are often confined to the universe of solutions within their own organization. External benchmarking encourages organizations to become more proactive—to "think out of the cubicle," as it were. Solutions abound in the marketplace: nonprofits learn best practices every day from businesses, governments, and other organizations. Rather than reinventing wheels or, worse, spinning wheels, you can

Benchmarking versus evaluation

Sometimes nonprofit managers confuse benchmarking with evaluation. The two concepts are related but quite distinct. Evaluation is traditionally applied only to programs, and seeks to prove causation (that a particular set of activities yielded a particular result, or outcome). Benchmarking, on the other hand, applies to all aspects of the organization—not just programs—and focuses on *improving results.* Benchmarkers seek to *improve* processes that drive results within an organization by measuring performance and applying best practices.

The difference between proving and improving is best illustrated by a simple example: the chicken crossing the road. Evaluation asks the question, How can you prove that the chicken got to the other side? Benchmarking asks the question, Assuming the chicken got to the other side, how fast did it walk, how far did it go, and how many feathers did it lose along the way? In short, evaluation investigates the underlying assumptions of why you are doing what you do, and focuses primarily on determining whether the results occurred. Benchmarking assumes that you already know what results you want, and focuses on improving your organization's ability to deliver those results.

we want to benchmark not evaluate

learn from others who have solved similar problems and put resources to work in the most efficient manner.

Again, remember that no organization can effectively benchmark against other organizations without first having a good gauge of its own performance.

Terminology

Terms such as *benchmark, continuous improvement,* and *best practice* have become quite common in casual nonprofit parlance. Sometimes they are used interchangeably by nonprofit practitioners, and often they are used to mean many different things. Before getting started, it is important to set some common definitions.

Baseline: an organization's *actual* or *current* level of results for a particular performance measure

Benchmark: an organization's *desired* level of results for a particular performance measure

Benchmarking: a systematic, continuous process of measuring and comparing an organization's business processes against leaders in any industry to gain insights that will help the organization take action to improve its performance

Best in Class: the most successful organization of a group based on its success in meeting or exceeding benchmarks relative to a particular outcome

Best Practice: the underlying innovation or lesson learned that enabled a high-performing organization to meet or exceed a benchmark (that is, achieve breakthrough performance)

Business Processes: a coordinated set of activities designed to produce certain outcomes (in nonprofits, processes can take the form of methods, policies, or programs)

Continuous Improvement: a constant, systematic cycle of identifying best practices and applying them within an organization to promote better performance

Critical to Quality Outcomes (also called CTQ outcomes): outcomes that are essential to the success of your organization—that is, if these things do not happen, your organization's impact will be substantially lessened

Effectiveness: the extent to which an organization succeeds at achieving the desired performance for its outcomes

Impact Area: one of four key components of a nonprofit organization's ultimate impact success—management effectiveness, financial sustainability, community engagement, or program performance

Outcome: a desired change in behavior or condition brought about by a particular set of activities or business processes

Performance Margin: the difference between an organization's actual performance results and those of the best in class

Performance Measure: a quantitative indicator that demonstrates how well a process achieves a particular outcome

Quality: the degree to which an organization has accomplished its outcomes and met the expectations of its stakeholders

Result: the actual throughput generated by an organization for a particular performance measure

Success Equation: a benchmarking tool that helps an organization define critical to quality outcomes and measures for each impact area

Theory of Change: an organization's strategy for solving a particular problem or bringing about a set of outcomes

Benefits of Benchmarking

Benchmarking offers numerous benefits to nonprofit managers. The process allows you to do the following:

Set high standards

Benchmarking teaches your organization to raise the bar higher. Rather than being limited to organic growth, organizations that benchmark learn to readjust their sights. They set goals proactively against top performers rather than reactively against internal standards. In this way, benchmarking infuses your organization with an optimistic, forward-thinking mind-set, comparing your performance to the best in class, or the "top of the line," as opposed to business as usual.

Sharpen your mission

In order to effectively compare your organization's performance to that of other organizations, you must have a keen understanding of what your organization *really* does (processes) and what it *really* wants to accomplish (outcomes). Imagine a theater trying to improve audience participation without knowing whether or not this is even important to the theater's mission. In this way, the process of benchmarking helps an organization focus on what matters while it improves its performance.

Raise more money

Benchmarking levels the playing field by allowing you to compete for funding based on your organization's effectiveness, not just on the people you know. Instead of relying on board contacts and the reputation of board members in the community, your organization can now present a more compelling reason for funders to support your cause: you are the best at what you do, and you can prove it.

Identify your strengths and weaknesses

The careful self-assessment that benchmarking requires also helps put into perspective what your organization is really good at, compared to other organizations, and where it needs improvement. Sometimes, you never know what you do well until you look at your performance in the context of how others are doing.

Build creativity into problem solving

A best-practice approach allows nonprofit managers to consider alternative ways of achieving their organization's mission. By directing your organization's decision makers to look outside their own unique experience, benchmarking encourages them to be more open-minded in considering solutions. This creativity infuses the entire organization with new ideas and fresh approaches to everyday problems.

Impress stakeholders

Organizations that demonstrate a commitment to tracking their results and improving on them impress both donors and constituents. Donors want to know that their contribution made a difference. Constituents want to know what results your organization can reliably deliver, and they will be drawn to a track record of success. Furthermore, the data that you gather—about your own organization and also about your competitors—will add a new dimension to your annual reports.

Common Concerns about Benchmarking

Nonprofit managers who haven't experienced benchmarking may express doubt about the process. Here are a few of the common reactions:

"But we're not a corporation"

Many nonprofit managers protest that benchmarking works only for businesses, that it is a "corporate" tool for management. What's more, some fear the "corporatizing" of the nonprofit sector and believe that emulating business practices compromises their organization's mission.

Benchmarking is an "organizational" process more than a "business" process. Therefore, benchmarking works in any organization that has a defined mission and goals and people working to achieve those goals.

"We can't afford it"

Smaller organizations (and even many larger ones) express concern that benchmarking is designed for larger organizations and seems too expensive. There's no extra funding for doing it, they say, and time is an even scarcer commodity than money. "How," they ask, "can we think about improving when we're just trying to survive?"

Benchmarking can be done at virtually no cost to your organization, and it actually saves time and money. Furthermore, you might not be able to afford not to do it. With competition intensifying and more nonprofits being created every day (approximately 150 on average[5]), just focusing on survival isn't going to cut it. If you're not able to thrive, you may not survive. Close to two-thirds of all nonprofits go out of business within ten years of their founding.[6] Benchmarking will help ensure that you are not one of them.

"We didn't invent it"

"We didn't invent it" and "But we're different" are common refrains heard among nonprofit staff when faced with implementing solutions that have worked elsewhere. It is often perceived that an "imported" solution is second rate because it was someone else's idea. Moreover, most nonprofit managers feel that their services and programs are unique and therefore no one else's solutions "fit" their organization's issues.

In fact, outside solutions probably won't interface perfectly with your problems. However, in benchmarking, as with shoe inserts, you must always trim around the edges to make a solution fit before you put it in place. Furthermore, while your organization's services may be distinct, odds are that its goals (or issues in achieving those goals) are not. The strength of benchmarking is that it embraces "difference"— learning from the "gap" between what one organization does versus another.

"Who are we to say what's the 'best'?"

Sometimes nonprofit managers express concern about their ability to judge what is "best." Further, many will respond that "best" is all relative and that no one person can possibly determine what is best for an entire industry.

Recall that the "best" in best practices applies more to what is "best" for your own organization than it does to finding the "holy grail" of solutions. Furthermore, by putting a benchmarking team in place, benchmarking yields a collective judgment that uses the best measures available to judge performance.

---

[5] According to IRS data, an average of 55,000 new 501(c)(3) organizations are created per year.

[6] Jed Emerson, "The U.S. Nonprofit Capital Market," NCCS Core Files 1990–2000, McKinsey Analysis.

"We're stealing other people's ideas"

Some managers question the ethics of benchmarking. They question whether one should snoop around other people's organizations, trying to co-opt their strategies and ideas.

Benchmarking is done informally every day by nonprofit organizations based on public information. When you read about a good idea in an industry publication or hear about an interesting new approach at a conference, you are also emulating other people's ideas. The point is that the focus should be on the positive: how can organizations come together and share ideas or solutions to more aggressively solve society's problems? Besides, benchmarking cannot be done without the cooperation of "partner" organizations, who often are flattered that you find their ideas innovative.

"We're already using a logic model"

The United Way and other funders sometimes require grantees to complete a logic model for their programs. These organizations may be concerned that benchmarking will somehow contradict or confuse that process.

A logic model expresses the organization's work and mission in terms of how the organization's resources and activities result in work products (or "outputs") that contribute various short-term to long-term outcomes—the changes they want to see happen in the world. Logic models are a visual and verbal expression of the organization's theory about how the work it does results in the impact it wants (its "theory of change"). The logic model is developed in part to figure out if what the organization says it is doing will really deliver the impact it wants to have. So one great use of the logic model is to check out whether the organization is doing the right things to accomplish its mission—that is, the logic model helps the organization challenge itself about its practices. Logic models are thus an important component of evaluating an organization's performance, and indeed they do overlap with benchmarking. (If your organization is unfamiliar with logic models, learn about them; they are an important tool. A simple explanation is included in the publication The Manager's Guide to Program Evaluation *by Paul Mattessich.[7] The* W.K. Kellogg Foundation Evaluation Handbook *includes detailed information on using logic models.[8])*

Are best practices always "best"?

The term "best practices" is often misunderstood in a nonprofit context. First of all, there is no such thing as a one-size-fits-all "best practice" for every organization. All best practices are relative—what is the best for one organization may be the worst for another. For example, conducting a board retreat may work well for one organization as a way to energize board members, but to another organization, board retreats may be time-wasting and counterproductive. The point is, a best practice is not a "correct" way of doing something. If anything, benchmarking demonstrates that many different best practices, or underlying innovations, explain breakthrough performance. Nonprofit managers should be careful to use the term only in the context of benchmarking. Some managers prefer to soften "best practices" by substituting "promising practices" or "better practices," but for purposes of this book, the term "best practices" will be used as defined in the section What Are Best Practices? on page 3.

---

[7] Paul Mattessich, *The Manager's Guide to Program Evaluation* (Saint Paul, MN: Fieldstone Alliance, 2003).

[8] W.K. Kellogg Foundation, *W.K. Kellogg Foundation Evaluation Handbook* (Battle Creek, MI: W.K. Kellogg Foundation, 1998), http://www.wkkf.org/Pubs/Tools/Evaluation/Pub770.pdf.

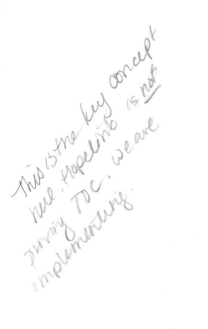
This is the key concept here. Hopelink is not ... TOC. We are implementing.

Benchmarking is related to logic models, but is more limited in scope. Benchmarking is not concerned with evaluating whether what the organization does contributes to its mission. Rather, benchmarking starts with the assumption that the organization's logic model is just fine. It focuses on the back end of the logic model—the outcomes and impact—and it is concerned with measuring and improving the processes related to the outcomes most critical to the desired impact. Benchmarking challenges the organization to improve its processes, but it does not directly challenge the organization's thinking about how what it does results in its impact. So benchmarking is not going to interfere with an evaluation or disrupt an organization's logic model. It is going to help the organization get better at what it already is doing.

Summary

Benchmarking is a systematic, continuous process for measuring and improving performance. While benchmarking originated as a tool of the for-profit world, it has common sense applications in daily life for everyone. Best of all, it is especially suited to the needs of today's underfunded nonprofits because it can help them use resources differently to increase impact.

As a management tool, benchmarking can be applied to almost anything a nonprofit organization does. Methods, policies, and programs can all be compared with those of other organizations, nonprofit or not, and can even be benchmarked across departments within the same organization. Thus, benchmarking has many direct and indirect benefits: increasing the impact of mission-related activities, raising internal standards, improving performance, attracting more funding, uncovering (and fixing) hidden weaknesses, and overall, improving the public face of the organization.

Many nonprofits have already taken the benchmarking plunge. You'll learn more about some of them as you read this book. Moreover, you'll learn a concrete process you can apply to deliver benchmarking's considerable benefits to your nonprofit.

Let's begin!

CHAPTER 1

Prepare Your Organization

A few years ago the CEO of a community foundation asked a leading management consultant to speak to his senior management team about benchmarking. The CEO was not able to be at the kickoff meeting due to a last-minute conflict. The consultant decided to proceed anyway and presented the concept of benchmarking and how it could be applied to improve key areas of the organization's performance: endowment performance, administrative efficiency, program performance, and donor relations. In a matter of minutes, the meeting spiraled into a maelstrom. Everyone was offended. The CFO resented the implication that her investment performance was subpar; one of the senior program directors insisted that her twenty-five years of experience qualified her to know more than the consultant ever would about her field; the head of development resented the comparison to a financial services firm to identify ways of improving relations with donors, exclaiming, "But we're not a mutual fund!"

So what went wrong? The CEO as spear-carrier wasn't present to say why benchmarking was important to his organization, the staff felt threatened by a new way of doing things, and there were no directives from the board or donors driving the organization to improve. In short, the organization wasn't ready.

Getting started with benchmarking does not require an expert, sophisticated tools, or a management training course. And you don't need to wait until your organization conducts a strategic plan or hires an evaluation guru. The reality is, successful benchmarking starts with a mandate to improve and the commitment to follow through. In Step 1, you will

- Assess organizational readiness
- Identify your mandate to improve
- Commit to quality
- Form a benchmarking team
- Assemble benchmarking resources
- Write a benchmarking plan

Step 1A: Assess Organizational Readiness

To begin benchmarking, your organization (or department) must be *ready* to improve. What does being ready mean? Principally, two things: first, commitment; and second, preparation. To be successful, you need both. A really committed organization that is not well prepared will not get far, nor will a really well-prepared organization with no commitment to follow through.

Worksheet 1: Readiness Checklist can help you assess your organization's readiness to tackle benchmarking.

Worksheet 1: Readiness Checklist

Check each question that applies to your organization.

- ❑ Is someone outside your organization (funders, competitors, partners) driving you to improve performance?   Y

- ❑ Is someone within your organization willing to champion process improvement?   Y

- ❑ Does your organization have chronic problems that are affecting the success of your mission?   Y

- ❑ Does your senior management believe that the organization is underperforming in certain areas?   Y

- ❑ Is your organizational culture open to change?   Y

- ❑ Are there consequences for your organization (or its staff) if change does not occur within the next twelve months?   ?

- ❑ Is staff compensation tied to performance?   N

- ❑ Has your board made "excellence" or "quality" an organizational priority?   Y

If you checked off at least six of the eight questions, odds are your organization is ready. If not, use these questions as readiness guideposts for your organization.

Step 1B: Identify Your Mandate to Improve

It may seem difficult to focus on trying to improve when many of today's nonprofits are struggling just to survive. Indeed, 60 percent of today's organizations will be out of business within ten years of their founding.[9] So who has time for benchmarking (that is, improving) when many organizations are just trying to stay afloat? The answer is that the only way to survive as a nonprofit in today's market is to *thrive*. With so many organizations seeking the same dollars, only the best will make it.

Absent a mandate to improve, your organization will not be successful in benchmarking. A mandate can come from outside your organization (funders or competitors) or from within (board or management). Here are the three most common drivers that lead organizations to want to benchmark.

1. **Market Drivers:** Today's funders are requiring better information on how well their money was spent—not just whether it was spent. Look at the trends: many community foundations now require grantees to measure the impact of their grants, United Ways require outcome measures, government agencies require performance data, and donors do more due diligence before they give.

   As discussed earlier, increased nonprofit competition is also driving practitioners to demonstrate and improve their organizations' results. See the section So Why Bother? on page viii.

   Benchmarking empowers nonprofit managers to take control of accountability and answer funders on their organizations' terms. By benchmarking, a nonprofit organization can define the terms of its own success. Benchmarking allows nonprofits to tell the market the other half of the story—what impact they made and why.

2. **Mission Drivers:** A mission statement is a road map to the future. One aspect of the organization's fiduciary duty is the duty of obedience. This duty requires that board members be faithful to the organization's mission. This is more than just avoiding waste; it means that board members are not permitted to act in a way that is inconsistent with the central goals of the organization.[10] Implicit in this fiduciary duty is a moral duty to maximize impact. Nonprofit organizations, and those that fund them, are in business to make an educational or charitable impact. Absent a profit motive, the nonprofit sector has an implicit motivation to seek the greatest "performance margin" possible.

   A well-known philanthropist tells the story of an Armenian charity he considered supporting. The organization provided winter coats to poor children in Armenia.

---

[9] Jed Emerson, "The U.S. Nonprofit Capital Market," NCCS Core Files 1990–2000, McKinsey Analysis.

[10] BoardSource, "Board Essentials," http://www.boardsource.org/ FullAnswerasp?ID=103.

He noted that the organization purchased coats at Wal-Mart for $30 per coat and that, with its limited budget of $1 million, was only able to clothe about 33,000 children. He did some research (benchmarking) and found that if the nonprofit purchased "second-run" coats at Burlington Coat Factory for $20 per coat, it could clothe 50,000 children with the same budget. The investor threatened to give his money to another charity if the organization didn't maximize its mission by operating more efficiently. Benchmarking ensures that your organization is always operating at peak performance.

3. **Management Drivers:** Nonprofit managers themselves are raising the bar by demanding better performance from their programs, internal accountability from their teams, and high standards for their organizations. In fact, a recent survey of organizations that are measuring their program results found that 61 percent of the organizations surveyed were prompted to measure by professional staff and leadership (as opposed to funders).[11]

Benchmarking can be used in nonprofit organizations to reduce employee turnover, improve morale, inspire innovation, and motivate staff to achieve more. Peter Drucker's famous phrase "You can't manage what you can't measure" is as relevant to nonprofit management as it is in business.[12] And more importantly, odds are your staff are already doing it. Almost daily, staff pick up new ideas at conferences, in trade journals, in discussions with peers, and on the Internet. An enormous amount of information is constantly being brought into your organization. Properly deployed, this information has the potential to significantly improve your organization's performance and get you closer to realizing your mission. But without a context—a proactive process for collecting, digesting, and assimilating information into knowledge—this information remains as random data. It is filling up file drawers, sitting on library shelves, embedded in research memos, and stored in people's heads. Benchmarking helps you harness the flow of information and use it to maximize your organization's impact.

✔ **TASK:** *Identify Your Organization's Mandate to Improve Performance*

---

[11] United Way of America, *Agency Experiences with Outcome Measurement*, Item Number 0196 (January 2000): 4.

[12] Peter F. Drucker, *Managing the Non-Profit Organization: Principles and Practices* (New York: HarperBusiness, 1992).

Q **SAMPLE**

Mandate to Improve

Here is a sample analysis of a mandate to improve from a community development corporation.

1. Key Market Drivers:
   - Government grants require us to report results.
   - Foundations are asking us to track outcomes.
   - Community development grants are increasingly competitive.

2. Key Mission Drivers:
   - Improving the capacity of community development corporations to deliver more extends our mission.
   - The more efficient we are, the more technical assistance we can provide.

3. Key Management Drivers:
   - Our capacity building initiative seeks to improve management practices.
   - Our board is committed to achieving maximum results.
   - The executive director has set performance and quality as a priority.

Now try Worksheet 2 to identify your organization's mandate to improve.

Worksheet 2: Mandate to Improve

Fill in the key drivers leading your organization to benchmark.

1. [Your Organization] _____'s Key **Market Drivers**:

   _____

   _____

   _____

2. [Your Organization] _____'s Key **Mission Drivers**:

   _____

   _____

   _____

3. [Your Organization] _____'s Key **Management Drivers**:

   _____

   _____

   _____

Step 1C: Commit to Quality

The first thing an organization (or department) must do to initiate benchmarking is to commit to being the best it can be—what benchmarkers call best in class. While that may seem implicit in your mission, making that commitment explicit rallies your organization and staff to elevate the game. It permeates every decision, action, and strategy with the question, How is this going to make us better, more efficient, and more impactful in what we do? A commitment to quality also means a commitment to continuous improvement and sends a signal to staff, board, and funders that your organization has set its sights on being a high performer.

The board, staff, and funders all need to take this "pledge." Everyone should know what is expected of them and agree to support the organization in undertaking this new process. Here are some highlights:

Role	Responsibilities
Management and staff	• Be open to new ideas • Collect data or research new ideas • Allocate time necessary for benchmarking • Be willing to learn from others
Board	• Make benchmarking a priority • Support the management team • Dedicate resources to accomplish benchmarking • Allocate time to implement new ideas
Funders	• Agree on performance measures • Provide resources if necessary • Reward progress and improvement • Encourage other grantees to share best practices

The Easter Seals Commits to Benchmarking sample, page 19, illustrates one organization's formal commitment to be the best it can be.

Note that a commitment to quality also requires a healthy dose of humility. As in the case with the community foundation described at the beginning of this chapter, fearing change, staffers may trot out an endless array of excuses for why they don't need to do any better. (See the section Common Concerns about Benchmarking on page 9.) It takes a strong, organization-wide commitment and an open mind to seek better ways of accomplishing an outcome. Leadership plays a critical role in focusing the organization on quality and inspiring staff to commit to achieving it.

✔ **TASK:** *Commit Your Organization to Quality*

Q SAMPLE

Easter Seals Commits to Benchmarking

In 1999, Easter Seals, a national organization that provides services to children and adults with disabilities and their families, made an organization-wide commitment to quality. Below is an excerpt from the Easter Seals Quality Charter.

EASTER SEALS QUALITY COUNCIL OPERATING CHARTER

I. PURPOSE

The purpose of the Quality Council is to collaborate with national headquarters to assist affiliates in the implementation of their quality journey through the application of quality practices and principles:

- Provide affiliates with a comprehensive set of resources and methods, in addition to the Landscape for Excellence (LFE) document, to implement and maintain their quality journey
- Provide education as to the value of quality to affiliates
- Offer affiliates a standardized, consistent method of comparing assessment scores with their own baseline data, and with other affiliates
- Encourage affiliate feedback and sharing of information regarding quality

The Vice President of Affiliate Services has responsibility for managing the day-to-day operations of Easter Seal quality policies, procedures, and plans.

II. QUALITY COUNCIL RESPONSIBILITIES

The Quality Council is responsible for the following:

- Marketing, communicating, and promoting a commitment to quality throughout Easter Seals
- Ongoing review, revision, and development of tools and processes provided to affiliates to assess and enhance quality of services and operations
- Providing affiliate perspective regarding quality issues to national headquarters
- Providing an open forum to discuss current Easter Seals quality initiatives both at national headquarters and affiliate level
- Providing recommendations regarding the Quality Council membership and leadership to the President and CEO of Easter Seals

III. SCHEDULE OF ACTIVITIES

The Quality Council will meet routinely via at least one annual face-to-face meeting and teleconferences as needed.

OUTCOME	GOAL	ACTION	STATUS (1/23/04)	ASSIGNMENTS
1. Affiliates are provided a comprehensive approach to implement quality practices	1. Identify required performance standards within the LFE	a. Examine membership agreement and board policies for required items and determine if they are in LFE, such as: audit, annual report, six-month financials, IRS 990s, accreditation, brand/name. Use analysis to develop a check-list that could be extracted from LFE.	COMPLETED	

(continued)

SAMPLE (continued)

OUTCOME	GOAL	ACTION	STATUS (1/23/04)	ASSIGNMENTS
1. Affiliates are provided a comprehensive approach to implement quality practice (continued)	2. Enhance use and value of LFE in a structured approach to quality improvement	b. Develop supplemental materials to support integration of LFE in quality improvement program. Elements may include: value of quality & LFE, FAQs re: LFE, timelines, examples of how to score and use of results, descriptive evidence of how indicators are met.	COMPLETED Links added from LFE to other resource material; still need ongoing maintenance plan and plan for adding other resources	J and R develop plan for ongoing maintenance of quality site
	3. Review and revise LFE	c. Write Board Development and Environment sections. d. Establish process for ongoing review and revision of LFE to include: adding new relevant categories, editing, and raising the bar.	COMPLETED New categories added and review completed; written process developed	Approve LFE review process
2. Organization-wide commitment to quality	1. Internally focused marketing/communication plan 2. Established national HQ practices to support commitment to quality	a. Develop a plan to raise awareness of quality and tools and practices to support quality. b. Develop QC history and transition book.	JS met with team in Feb.; preliminary communication plan discussed; surveyed affiliates at NTC; formal communication plan under construction; several elements complete	R, J, and JS
3. Vehicles to share best practices throughout the organization	1. Training	a. Establish process for feedback to training team using LFE summary results to identify training needs. b. Develop process for LFE /quality orientation for new staff.	LFE added to new CEO orientation; PPT on extranet site; LFE in new NHQ employee orientation; KP organize 2 infoshare teleconferences for FY04 P, R, and J develop training presentation and pilot at Mideast meeting in Sept. 03	
	2. Resource library	c. Extranet site (see Goal 1, Training). d. Collect best practices samples internally and externally.	Not done	C develop recommendations for process to collect best practice
	3. Recognition	e. Incorporate recognition of quality in existing national awards. f. Develop informal recognition vehicles.	Executive Office open to new ideas; QC to make recommendations	On hold for FY 04
4. Method for comparison of quality measures across affiliates	1. Data collection and analysis to identify training, potential trainers, best practices, raising bar, etc.	a. Pilot collection of aggregate LFE data. b. Develop implementation plan and identify resources needed for ongoing data collection, comparisons, summaries and analysis.	Data reviewed in Feb 03	P and E participate in benchmarking project

Step 1D: Form a Benchmarking Team

For many reasons, most organizations find it helpful to put together a benchmarking team to direct and carry out the benchmarking process, secure the necessary resources, and commit the time to get the job done.

First, there needs to be buy-in from different players inside the organization. Having stakeholders on the team engages them in the process and helps to ensure support of the outcomes. Second, the team needs different competencies. Interdisciplinary groups are often the most effective. Individuals should be chosen by their role in the organization as well as their skill sets. Members can be drawn from development, marketing, program, and finance departments. Sometimes having a board member, a constituent, or a volunteer involved is also useful, as these people can provide a more objective perspective. You want a group that has management experience as well as day-to-day contact with the people you serve. You also need some people who can work well with data, some people who are outgoing and comfortable contacting outsiders, and some people who are able to set priorities internally to make sure that new ideas get properly implemented. This usually ends up including accountants, managers, instructors, and researchers, to mention a few. The team should still be manageable in size, usually around three to five people, depending on the size of the organization—so clearly, you need to find people who combine the qualities mentioned above.

At Easter Seals, the Quality Team is serious stuff (see the sample on page 24). Membership requires a two-year commitment and draws from executive management, from the information technology, finance, programs, and human resources departments, and from over ninety affiliates. A team leader is designated by the CEO to serve a one-year term. In addition, team members must have "a demonstrated commitment to quality and sufficient time to devote" to the team. Of course, most nonprofits are much smaller and won't require such formality. But the point is, the team needs to commit to this work for long enough to change the processes that will be benchmarked.

> **TIP: Make sure leadership is committed**
>
> Be sure the top people in the group that will be benchmarking have committed to the process. If the benchmarking is going to be organization-wide, top management needs to make the commitment. If it is a department or smaller organization, the lead people or entire team should make the commitment. Whether you make a formal commitment or simply rally the troops, be sure the relevant leadership in your organization is committed to the effort.

Step 1E: Assemble Benchmarking Resources

Once your organization (or department) has made the commitment to improve and begun to assemble the human resources, you will need to also assemble the physical resources necessary to benchmark. These include the essential tools you'll need to get through the project and collect, manage, and synthesize the information.

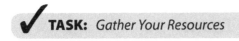 **TASK:** *Gather Your Resources*

Worksheet 3: Benchmarking Resources has a list of the necessary tools. Use it to help you gather your resources.

Worksheet 3: Benchmarking Resources

Use the following checklist to make sure you are prepared for benchmarking.

❑ **Computer**

You'll need a computer to document the plan, keep track of progress, store information, and access the Internet. Ideally, your team should have access to at least one laptop computer for taking notes at meetings.

❑ **Database**

You'll need some basic software to keep track of information. A simple database or spreadsheet will do, such as Microsoft Access® or Excel®. There are also more sophisticated databases such as Microsoft Project® and even specialized benchmarking software for nonprofits. Centralized access, either through a network or via the web, is ideal. More information about selecting a software program can be found in Appendix B.

❑ **Strategic plan (or a mission statement or department goals)**

This will help when you are analyzing areas for improvement. If you do not have a strategic plan, a mission statement or list of departmental goals will suffice.

❑ **Internet**

A web connection provides access to the most efficient and cost-effective research vehicle: the Internet. The Internet also provides an anonymous means of learning about other organizations without having to speak to anyone.

❑ **Guide**

If you are a first-time benchmarker, you will likely need a guide to walk you through the process. This will help you stay focused, ensure the inquiry is successful, and make the most efficient use of your time. A guide can be a book, such as this one, or a consultant.

❑ **Budget**

While benchmarking doesn't have to cost a lot, it can involve some incidental expenses. Travel, photocopying, meetings, technology, and consultants can all be used in benchmarking and require your organization to think through your budget before proceeding.

Step 1F: Write a Benchmarking Plan

Think of benchmarking as you would a research project. The benchmarking plan is your research proposal, your road map. It tells why you are undertaking the research and sets out the scope of the project: what you want to benchmark, how long it's going to take, who will be involved, and what results you expect. A benchmarking plan usually has four sections:

1. **Purpose:** Why are we doing this? What outcome are we expecting to improve?

2. **Scope:** What are the critical areas for improvement? What are the specific processes (methods, policies, or programs) that we want to benchmark?

3. **Logistics:** What resources are we going to need? How much time are we going to dedicate? Who needs to be involved? Where will we get the data?

4. **Deliverables:** What should the project produce? Should recommendations be in the form of best practices, prescriptions for change, benchmark statistics? Who should read the findings?

Invariably, your plan will need to balance flexibility and "scope creep." Flexibility allows you to adjust the scope when you find that your initial inquiry is misguided or unproductive. Scope creep happens when a benchmarking inquiry becomes too broad and loses focus. Assume your purpose (outcome) is to improve constituent satisfaction. You may end up determining that the processes you thought you needed to benchmark—fielding constituent inquiries, responding with the right information, training the people answering the phones—were not the key drivers. It may turn out that the problem with constituent satisfaction really lies in the quality of your product or service itself. A balanced plan flexes enough to readjust your benchmarking scope to include this new variable; but at the same time it will keep you from getting sidetracked with too many new variables.

TASK: *Draft Your Benchmarking Plan* ✔

Many organizations will create a formal benchmarking charter, similar to the Easter Seals charter shown on pages 24–25. Use Worksheet 4: Benchmarking Charter, page 26, to complete your own charter.

Q SAMPLE

Easter Seals Benchmarking Charter

EASTER SEALS BENCHMARKING PROJECT CHARTER
(Updated September 2003)

Sponsor: Jim Williams

Team Leader: Donna Davidson, CEO North Georgia

Team Members: Brian Fitzgerald, CEO New Jersey
Elin Treanor, CFO New Hampshire/New York
Pat Jones, VP Affiliate Services
Joanne Cloonan, Project Manager, National Headquarters
Jason Saul, Consultant B2P

1. Project Vision and Purpose:

The purpose of this project is to improve affiliate performance and support affiliate growth through a process that identifies standards of excellence or benchmarks that contribute to healthy mission-driven growth. The vision is that knowledge gained from benchmarking will enable Easter Seals to deliver more services by building affiliate capacity. The intent is to provide affiliates with a means of assessing their current capacity for sustainability and growth, and guidance in planning and implementing growth strategies. Affiliates will increase effectiveness by learning from the successes of others. Best practices (successful innovations or techniques of other top-performing organizations) that support enhanced performance and organizational growth will be determined and shared system-wide.

Desired outcomes of the project include affiliates gaining a better understanding of what it will take to grow their organization to the next level, and national headquarters having another means to design and prioritize the delivery of resources to affiliates to enhance affiliate capacity building. Benchmarking successful affiliates will also compliment other initiatives underway to develop program standards and support continuous quality improvement in all aspects of Easter Seals operations.

2. What specific tasks are those involved in this project going to accomplish?

a. Overall project design
b. Organizational education and training
c. Data collection, measurement
d. Analysis and identification of benchmarks
e. Identification of best practices
f. Report of key findings and recommendations

3. Describe the point of completion for this project:

a. __X__ Complete the project deliverables and hand them off to others to implement and sustain.
b. ____ Implement and sustain the project deliverables.

SAMPLE (continued)

4. Describe the scope or boundaries for this project.

Completion schedule: report and training at Nationwide Training Conference, April '04

Affected NHQ departments: Affiliate Services, DM/Dev. Services, Exec, Finance, HR, IT, MCR, and PPS

Regional or National Scope: both, collaborative project with ESLA

Cost parameters: staff time, conference calls and travel integration with other NHQ initiatives: Interdepartmental Goals, Program Service Line Standards, Peer Group Analysis, Quality Council, AS Dept. Goals

Participation/representation outside NHQ: ESLA Board representatives and select affiliates

5. What resources are necessary for this project to be successful?

Number of people/Time required

5 team members: 3 affiliates, 2 NHQ	Minimum 20 hours each in preparation conference calls as needed
	6 days travel and meetings (3 meetings)
6 focus group affiliates	2 hours preparation and 2 days travel and meetings
Number of affiliates participating in data collection: (TBD)	
NHQ departments and staff: (TBD)	

Budget

Focus group meeting, July '03
Conference calls
Team travel and meetings: 2 face-to-face meetings (Oct and TBD)
Consultant

6. How will the department heads and other project leads stay informed and engaged with this project? What is the forum for project status?

Briefings to sponsor, Mteam, and ESLA officers through calls and e-mail; minutes of meetings will be sent to those above and update communications to other individuals and affiliates involved from time to time throughout the course of the project.

7. Where will project updates be sent? How will they be accessible to others?

E-mails sent to group above may be circulated to others as determined by the team leader and sponsor and incorporated into Mteam and ESLA meeting agendas.

Worksheet 4: Benchmarking Charter

Use this worksheet as a basis for writing your benchmarking plan.

Sponsor _____

Team Members

Name [last, first]	Department [Select from: finance, human resources, programs, marketing, development, executive, or board]	Skill Set [Select from: detail oriented, relationship builder, business savvy, creative thinker, process expert, or leader]

Project Vision and Purpose _____

_____

_____

_____

Deliverables

a._____

b._____

c._____

d._____

e._____

Timeline

Project Kickoff Date: _____, 20_____

Milestones	Due Dates

(continued)

Worksheet 4 continued

Scope

Completion schedule: _____, 20_____

Participating departments: _____

_____

Cost parameters: _____

_____

_____

Integration with other initiatives: _____

_____

External participation/representation: _____

_____

Resources

Number of people/Time required: _____

_____

Budget: _____

_____

_____

_____

Resources needed: _____

_____

Potential funding sources: _____

_____

_____

Communications

Frequency (weekly, monthly, quarterly): _____

Communications lead (name of team member): _____

Format (e-mail, newsletter, conference call, meeting): _____

_____

Summary

Organizations are driven to benchmark by the market (competition is driving nonprofits to demonstrate and improve their results), by their mission (an organization's duty to maximize its impact), or by management (nonprofit managers themselves are raising the bar). But in order for benchmarking to be successful, your organization needs to have both a mandate to improve and a commitment to follow through.

Your organization's board, staff, volunteers, and funders all need to commit to benchmarking and understand their roles in supporting the process. Without this commitment, an organization often goes through the process of benchmarking but stops short of implementing the findings. Creating a benchmarking team helps rally buy-in from different stakeholders inside the organization and ensures that people with different perspectives and expertise will be involved in decision making. A benchmarking plan is the benchmarking team's road map: it tells the reason why you are undertaking the research and sets the scope of the project. Writing the plan in a formal charter will help keep the project focused and on track.

The benchmarking team's first step is to analyze what needs to be improved. Chapter 2 will help you determine what to benchmark.

> **TIP: Have fun with it**
>
> Benchmarking is serious business, but it can also be a lot of fun. The process allows people to get out of old routines, be creative, and even travel. One of the most valuable by-products of benchmarking is energy and creativity. Allow your staff the freedom to go with the flow—to seek out and explore new ideas. Encourage discussion and interaction among different levels of the organization around alternative solutions. A process that is enjoyable and engaging will be more productive, and better received, than one that is not.

CHAPTER 2

Analyze What to Improve

In every organization, dozens of things can be benchmarked and improved. The question is always where to start. The key to answering this question lies in understanding what "quality" means for each aspect of your organization. In corporate benchmarking, quality is defined by how well the company meets the customer's expectations. In nonprofit benchmarking, quality means *successfully achieving your organization's outcomes.* Of course, there are always impediments that prevent your organization from achieving its outcomes. Every organization that has outcomes has these impediments. Benchmarking can help you to identify and overcome impediments to meeting organizational outcomes and improve quality.

Once you've made a commitment to improve, prepared your team, and gathered your resources, you can move on to the next step: sorting out what to benchmark. In Step 2, you will

- Determine what needs to be improved
- Identify your critical to quality outcomes
- Build your own success equation

Step 2A: Determine What Needs to Be Improved

In smaller organizations, as in larger ones, there are always too many things that need to be fixed. But fixing everything isn't the answer. The key is fixing the right things. Your benchmarking team should focus on improving those things that help bring your organization closer to its ultimate success—that is, those outcomes that matter most to your mission. As you think about the different dimensions of success for your organization, keep in mind the four impact areas in nonprofit organizations: management effectiveness, financial sustainability, community engagement, and program performance.

The **management effectiveness** impact area relates to the way your organization is managed. How engaged is your board? What is employee satisfaction like? Do you have high turnover? Do you have a quality management team?

The **financial sustainability** impact area relates to the long-term financial success of your organization. How stable is your organization financially? How diversified are your revenue streams? Are your donors or funders renewing each year?

The **community engagement** impact area relates to the visibility of your organization among its constituents. Are constituents aware of your programs? How well does your organization promote itself within its target community? Are local volunteers engaged? What is the quality of your brand?

The **program performance** impact area relates to the success of your programs toward achieving your mission. What behaviors must be changed, what conditions must be ameliorated, or what skills must be improved to bring about the ultimate goals of your programs?

TIP: Focus on the "customer"

The customer usually determines quality standards. Who is the customer? For businesses, the answer is easy—the customer is the consumer of the product or service. But for nonprofit organizations, identifying who the "customer" is (and therefore who determines "quality") isn't always that straightforward. For example, is your customer the foundation that's giving you the grant to do your work, the government agency that's regulating your service delivery, or the constituent who is benefiting from your services? The truth is, nonprofit organizations have multiple customers, or "stakeholders." The careful balancing of those different stakeholder expectations will determine how your organization defines "quality."

These four impact areas make up the fundamental components of an organization's success. Begin by selecting one impact area your organization would like to improve and declare an impact goal you would like to achieve. For instance, an organization designed to end homelessness might decide to work on program performance, choosing "constituent employment" as its overall impact goal.

From here, your benchmarking team will build a success equation for your organization, allowing you to (1) translate your organization's overarching mission into impact areas; (2) identify key outcomes to focus on; and (3) attach measures to your outcomes. The success equation will help you focus your efforts and establish what you need to benchmark to ultimately improve your organization.

Often, trying to measure long-term goals for your organization can be challenging. This is because change frequently takes place over time (that is, the impact is "longitudinal"). As described in the section What Do You Benchmark, pages 4–5, long-term impacts fall into four areas: management, financial, community, or programmatic. The success equation helps you quickly break down your long-term impact into manageable components. Basically, it is as simple as: $A + B + C = D$. D is the impact goal that is desired, and A, B, and C are the intermediate outcomes that most directly contribute to your ultimate goal. If you've done your success equation properly, you should be able to speak it as a complete sentence: "In order to ultimately succeed at D, we must accomplish A and B and C."

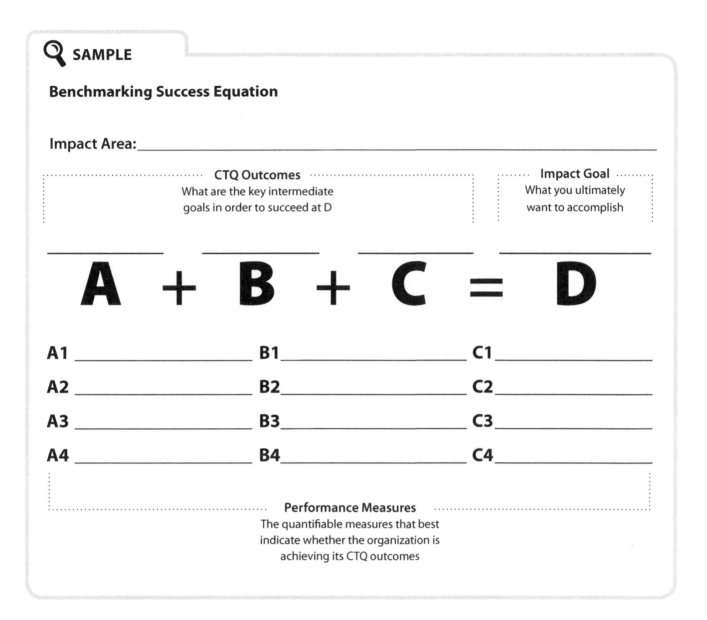

Try speaking this sentence for one of your impact areas. (Eventually, you will use a separate success equation for each impact area.)

Now that you have a general understanding of the success equation, it's time to choose an impact goal for you organization. The sidebar, TIP: Get Started with Simple Goals, gives some guidelines—but the most important thing now is to keep it simple. Learn to benchmark by starting with something relatively straightforward. For example, your impact goal could be to gain independence from foundation grants. This goal becomes *D* in the success equation. (By the way, if you choose "independence from foundation grants," you've chosen an impact goal within the impact area of financial sustainability.)

TIP: Get started with simple impact goals

Benchmarking is an ambitious undertaking. Success requires that your organization embrace new ideas and welcome outside input. At the same time, you want to be careful not to do too much. Here are some tips for selecting your first few projects.

Bite off only what you can chew. Start off by benchmarking one or two impact areas. Then, when the process gets more familiar, move on to other areas. Many organizations make the mistake of trying to introduce benchmarking throughout the entire organization before trying it out in a couple of key areas. Also, be realistic about the resources your organization can afford to devote to the benchmarking process. Your resources will govern the scope of your efforts: how far and wide you can look for ideas, and how carefully you can measure their effectiveness.

Don't try to boil the ocean. Remember that benchmarking focuses on short-term results. Therefore, avoid super-long-term outcomes. It's easy to come up with an amorphous, big-picture goal like "change the world." It takes more thought to break that goal down into measurable, controllable results that your organization can directly influence. Long-term outcomes (for example, eradicate racism, reduce poverty) are often driven by many complex processes and interactions—most of them out of your control. So focus on the outcomes that you can control.

Go for the low-hanging fruit. The first thing that comes to mind when most practitioners hear the term "outcome" is a programmatic goal. Program outcomes are usually the most mission-critical, but they are sometimes complex and confusing. So think about starting with outcomes that are more concrete and measurable. Outcomes in the financial or management impact areas, for instance, generally have clear business processes and fairly straightforward measures. Once you get the hang of it, you can move on to more challenging outcomes in the program and community impact areas.

✔ **TASK:** *Choose an Impact Goal*

It's time to choose *D* in your success equation. For your first project, pick something you understand well and can be successful at. Fill in the impact goal line on Worksheet 5, page 34.

Step 2B: Identify Your Critical to Quality Outcomes

The first step in building your success equation was to select the impact goal that you want to focus on for improvement through benchmarking—*D* in the success equation. Now it's time to look at what makes *D* happen.

For any impact goal, there are some intermediate outcomes that are critical to that goal's success. These key outcomes are called your critical to quality outcomes (or CTQ outcomes). These are outcomes that your organization must accomplish in order to make a difference in a particular impact area. To continue the example from the previous step, your organization wants to "gain independence from foundation grants." Various outcomes may be on your radar screen, such as getting more government grants, increasing the number of online donations, organizing high-visibility fundraising events, and growing earned-income streams. However, you might determine that the three most critical prerequisites to financial sustainability are obtaining government grants, increasing online donations, and improving earned-income streams. These will be your CTQ outcomes for the financial sustainability impact area. The example below now shows these CTQ outcomes filled out in the success equation.

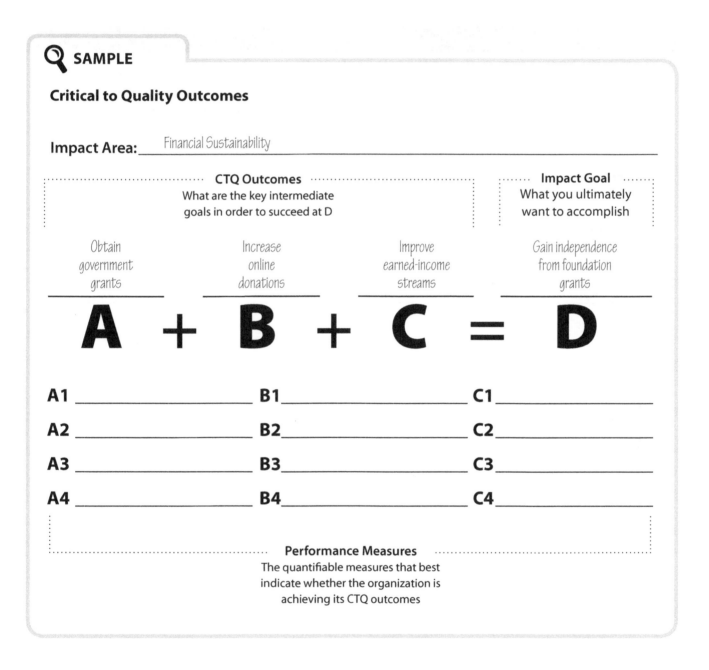

SAMPLE

Critical to Quality Outcomes

Impact Area: _Financial Sustainability_

················ **CTQ Outcomes** ················
What are the key intermediate
goals in order to succeed at D

········ **Impact Goal** ·······
What you ultimately
want to accomplish

| Obtain government grants | Increase online donations | Improve earned-income streams | Gain independence from foundation grants |

$$A \quad + \quad B \quad + \quad C \quad = \quad D$$

A1 _____ B1 _____ C1 _____

A2 _____ B2 _____ C2 _____

A3 _____ B3 _____ C3 _____

A4 _____ B4 _____ C4 _____

Performance Measures
The quantifiable measures that best
indicate whether the organization is
achieving its CTQ outcomes

✔ **TASK:** *List Your Critical to Quality Outcomes*

The purpose of this task is to help you identify your CTQ outcomes. Work with your benchmarking team to answer the questions in Worksheet 5: Benchmarking Diagnostic. Have each member of your team complete the worksheet independently and then compare notes. At the end, make sure the team reaches consensus, as the information identified in the worksheet will set the priorities for your benchmarking inquiry. For more tips, see the sidebar on page 36.

Worksheet 5: Benchmarking Diagnostic

With respect to your impact goal, list the top five to ten things about your organization that you feel most need improvement. For now, you should limit your brainstorming to the impact goal you selected at the end of Step 2A. (Eventually, you can fill out this worksheet for impact goals within each of the four impact areas. For now, just keep it simple.)

Impact Goal: _____

List of possible CTQ outcomes:

1. _____

2. _____

3. _____

4. _____

5. _____

6. _____

7. _____

8. _____

9. _____

10. _____

(continued)

Worksheet 5 continued

Take each item in the list and drop it into one of the quadrants in the matrix below. This matrix will help your team focus on the outcomes most critical to your organization's success. This matrix isolates outcomes that are important and controllable from those that are unimportant (that is, do not have a strong impact on quality) or uncontrollable (that is, cannot reasonably be affected by your organization).

Important/Controllable	**Important/Uncontrollable**
Unimportant/Controllable	**Unimportant/Uncontrollable**

The items you listed in the upper-left quadrant (important/controllable) are your CTQ outcomes for the impact goal you selected. They are the ones that you have determined are within your organization's ability to influence and matter the most to your organization's success.

If you find the team lists more than three outcomes that are important and controllable, try looking for overlap among goals; ask the team, "Does one of our goals really encompass another?" For example, CTQ outcomes listed as "improve donor database list sales" and "increase consulting revenues" can be captured together as "improve earned-income streams."

Use the success equation below to fill in the impact area and the related CTQ outcomes.

Impact Area:_____

CTQ Outcomes	Impact Goal
What are the key intermediate goals in order to succeed at D	What you ultimately want to accomplish

$$\text{A} + \text{B} + \text{C} = \text{D}$$

TIP: How to choose and state critical to quality outcomes

Here are a few tips to help you complete your success equation:

Confirm that your CTQ outcomes are shorter-term. All outcomes unfold in gradations: for example, people graduate from a class (short-term outcome), apply for jobs (intermediate-term outcome), take new jobs (long-term outcome), and become financially independent (ultimate impact). Shorter-term outcomes are more within your control to influence or change. The further out in time that a change occurs, the less ability you have to measure or control it.

Always use active verbs for CTQ outcomes. This is one way to make sure you come up with actual outcomes rather than processes or activities. Remember, an outcome—even an intermediate one—is a change in a condition, circumstance, or behavior. Active verbs (add, improve, engage, mobilize, increase) will help you define the change you wish to bring about and lead you to ask the right questions. One common mistake is to list activities (hiring a development officer, hosting a conference, interviewing a participant) instead of outcomes. Usually, activities do not indicate a change—they either happen or they don't. A good rule of thumb is this: if the CTQ outcome has a yes/no consequence rather than a matter of degree, it's probably an activity, and you should go back and identify an outcome.

Don't fret over causation. CTQ outcomes are only surrogates for determining what to focus on to improve your impact. The success equation cannot tell the whole story, and the CTQ outcomes will not be the only outcomes that contribute to the ultimate impact. Rather, CTQ outcomes should be the most important, direct ways of getting results that you want. Remember—benchmarking is about improving. So in building your success equation, you are trying to focus on the key outcomes that, if improved, will most likely lead to greater impact.

Step 2C: Attach Performance Measures

You've listed a series of critical outcomes—but knowing your CTQs isn't enough. Now you must find ways to measure them so you can determine how much you need to improve. These measurements are called *performance measures*. A performance measure is a quantitative indicator (usually numerical) that tracks how well a process (method, policy, or program) is achieving a desired outcome.

Of course, each of the outcomes you've designated has a set of processes that deliver the outcome. For example, if one CTQ is "obtain more government contracts," you are going to have to understand the methods you currently use to obtain those contracts. The performance measure you pick will be a number, but that number stands for the process itself. Later on, when you benchmark your organization against a better organization, you'll be comparing numbers—but more important, you'll be asking questions about just how that organization got the better numbers.

Picking performance measures can be difficult. Many businesses have simple, easy-to-measure processes, such as "unload and verify stock received from supplier A" and "put correct stock into inventory." However, nonprofits tend to have more complex processes. In the case of fundraising, it may be relatively simple to measure some items: "place a call to donor A; go through our standard three-asks structure starting with an amount ten times donor A's last contribution." But more complex processes involving government contracting, foundation relations, networking, and so forth, can be difficult to measure.

The benchmarking team should think of how it will measure progress toward the CTQ outcomes stated at the end of Step 2B. The measures could be quite straightforward: percent growth in contracts, cost per dollar of revenue earned, total contract value.

The sample on page 38 is a modified excerpt from one nonprofit's benchmarking initiative. It provides an example of how an organization measured its impact goal of achieving effective agency management. From the example, you can see that overall, the nonprofit is benchmarking the impact "Achieve effective agency management" (*D* in the success equation). One of the nonprofit's CTQ outcomes is "Develop effective leadership."

Study the example. You can see that this nonprofit measures progress toward the CTQ outcome "Develop effective leadership" in several ways. It determined that leadership can be indicated, or measured, by financial management (change in net assets ratio and program revenue growth) and by constructive human interaction (employee satisfaction and board participation). To the benchmarking team, these are all indicators of good leadership.

In preparation for developing your own performance measures, take some time as a group to study this example. Talk through how each of the performance measures relates to the particular CTQ outcome, and how the three CTQ outcomes add up to the overall impact goal. Further, think about processes the nonprofit might use to achieve each of the performance measures it is using to deliver each CTQ outcome. (You don't have to be "right"; you just have to use your imagination to connect the measures to processes that deliver those changes.) For more examples of common nonprofit performance measures and related outcomes see Appendix A, page 87.

For this example, we show only four measures for each CTQ outcome. Undoubtedly, the benchmarking team came up with many more measures it thought important to track. But remember to keep it manageable—you should not use more than three or four indicators per CTQ outcome. In fact, sometimes there may only be one or two good indicators, and that is fine.

SAMPLE

Performance Measures

Impact Area: _Management Effectiveness_

CTQ Outcomes
What are the key intermediate
goals in order to succeed at D

Impact Goal
What you ultimately
want to accomplish

Develop effective leadership	Support key functions	Ensure mission critical reporting	Achieve effective agency management

$$A \quad + \quad B \quad + \quad C \quad = \quad D$$

A1 Change in net assets ratio (%)

A2 Program revenue growth by function (%)

A3 Employee satisfaction rate (%)

A4 Board participation rate (%)

B1 HR FTEs as percent of all FTEs (%)

B2 Days elapsed per workstation incident (#)

B3 Marketing expense as percent of total (%)

B4 Hiring success rate 90 days retention (%)

C1 Bottom line financial reporting & analysis

C2 Achieved outcomes per dollar by reporting agency

C3 Leads converted to sales report (#)

C4 Results promised results achieved (%)

Performance Measures
The quantifiable measures that best
indicate whether the organization
is achieving its CTQ outcomes

✔ **TASK:** *Attach Performance Measures to Outcomes*

Use Worksheet 6: Performance Measures to attach performance measures to the critical to quality outcomes you've chosen.

Worksheet 6: Performance Measures

For each CTQ outcome listed in your success equation, list the relevant performance measures in the allotted columns of the worksheet below. For examples of typical performance measures and outcomes in nonprofit organizations, see Appendix A.

Impact Area:_____

CTQ Outcomes
What are the key intermediate
goals in order to succeed at D

Impact Goal
What you ultimately
want to accomplish

$$A \ + \ B \ + \ C \ = \ D$$

A1 _____   **B1** _____   **C1** _____

A2 _____   **B2** _____   **C2** _____

A3 _____   **B3** _____   **C3** _____

A4 _____   **B4** _____   **C4** _____

Performance Measures
The quantifiable measures that best
indicate whether the organization
is achieving its CTQ outcomes

Summary

Determining what to benchmark starts with understanding your organization's strengths and weaknesses and deciding what areas need improvement. From there, you determine the combination of critical to quality outcomes that contribute to your long-term impacts. You then establish performance measures that allow you to measure your progress toward these outcomes.

Your analysis will undoubtedly uncover a number of outcomes through which you deliver your work. It is up to your benchmarking team to identify and prioritize those outcomes that relate to the most essential components of your organization's performance.

In the next chapter, you will assess the measures you chose in this chapter, create internal baselines, and "calibrate" your organization's performance measures to those of other organizations.

CHAPTER 3

Measure Performance

For fifty years, the Nature Conservancy had a clear mission: "to preserve the diversity of plants and animals by protecting the habitats of rare species around the world." For most of the Conservancy's history, its focus was on "protecting habitats" (outcome). Year after year, the Conservancy would add up the amount of annual charitable donations it received (measure) and the number of acres it was protecting (measure). These measurements were commonly known as "bucks and acres." The measures were clear and easy to track. Year after year, the number of acres protected grew exponentially, from 200,000 acres in 1971 to 40 million in 1991 to 66 million in 1999. Meanwhile, the Conservancy's annual revenues also steadily increased each year, from $42.5 million in 1971 to $254.7 million in 1991 to $775 million in 1999. The organization was thriving and board, managers, and funders alike felt that it was at the top of its game.

Once you have identified the measures you want to benchmark, you can begin benchmarking performance. In Step 3, you will

- Be sure to measure the right thing
- Identify your baseline
- Set internal benchmarks for your measures

Despite this apparent success, in the early 1990s Conservancy managers began to realize that bucks and acres didn't adequately measure the progress of the organization toward achieving its mission. The Conservancy's goal, after all, wasn't to buy land or raise money; it was to preserve the diversity of life on Earth. And by that standard, the Conservancy had been falling short every year of its existence. In fact, species were declining at a rate as high as during the great extinction 65 million years ago! Even worse, species were even declining within the protected areas.[13]

Lesson learned: make sure you are measuring what matters. It's relatively easy to measure something. The key is measuring the *right* things.

---

[13] John Sawhill and David Williamson, "Measuring What Matters in Nonprofits," *The McKinsey Quarterly* 2 (2001): 100–101.

Step 3A: Be Sure to Measure the Right Thing

Step 3A is really about making sure your measures correlate directly to the outcomes you are trying to achieve.

To ensure you are selecting useful measures, strive for "SMART" measures.[14] SMART criteria are frequently used to determine the usefulness, validity, and accuracy of the performance measures. In order for a performance measure to be effective, it should be

Specific

The performance measure has to indicate exactly what result is expected so that the performance can be judged accurately. The specificity of the measure is aided by clear definitions and standards for data collection, standardization, and reporting across departments and among employees involved in use of the measurement.

Measurable

The intended result has to be something that can be measured and reported in quantitative and/or clear qualitative terms. This characteristic is achieved when programs set numeric targets or employ an evaluative approach that can ascertain in a definitive manner whether performance expectations have been met.

Accountable

The performance measure has to be "owned" by a specific business line or employee base to the degree that someone, or some group, is held accountable for the performance measure to ensure that the results are indeed produced. Accountability is more than clarifying who is charged with achieving the result; it requires that management has devised targets based on what reasonably can be produced by the program during a given period of time. Accountability cannot be achieved if targets are unreasonable from the start.

Results-oriented

The performance measure must be aligned to the outcome and track an important value or benefit needed to advance the strategies and achieve the end results of the organization: mission impact. A performance measurement meets this test if it (1) measures an end or intermediate outcome or (2) links to a process or activity that, if successful, will achieve an outcome.

Time-bound

The performance measure must set a specific time frame for the results to be produced as well as allow for the reporting of performance in a timely manner. In this case, the organization must have measures to provide fresh enough data to be used by management for adjustments in the program and corrective action if necessary.

---

[14] Adapted from the American Strategic Management Institute, http://www.managementweb.org/methodology.htm.

TASK: *"SMART-Check" Your Performance Measures*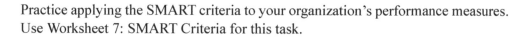

Practice applying the SMART criteria to your organization's performance measures.
Use Worksheet 7: SMART Criteria for this task.

Worksheet 7: SMART Criteria

List your organization's performance measures (determined in Step 2C) in the left-hand column. Then apply the SMART criteria to each measure by filling in the appropriate column. If you are unable to apply a particular criterion, you will need to do more planning for the measure or, possibly, select a different measure. (If you need to select a different measure, return briefly to Step 2C; be sure the measure attaches directly to one of your CTQ outcomes.)

| | SMART Criteria | | | | |
Performance Measure	**Specific** (indicate whether a benchmark has been set)	**Measurable** (indicate %, #, $, Yes/No)	**Accountable** (indicate name of measure owner)	**Results-Oriented** (indicate related outcome)	**Time-Bound** (indicate frequency of measurement availability: weekly, monthly, quarterly, annually)

And one last thing: while the goal is always to identify the right measures, the simple process of struggling with performance measurement can be transformative in and of itself, as the following quote illustrates:

> *The simple act of defining measures is extremely enlightening to many organizations. When [public agencies] have to define the outcomes they want and the appropriate benchmarks to measure those outcomes, this confusion is forced into the open. People begin to ask the right questions, to redefine the problem they are trying to solve, and to diagnose that problem anew.*[15]

Step 3B: Collect Internal Data to Set a Baseline

Once you've identified performance measures, the next task is to determine what performance data your organization currently tracks and how reliable that information is. You will learn a lot about where information gaps (that is, outdated or unavailable information) are in your organization just by looking for data.

Performance data can be found in many places within your organization—not always in a tidy, centralized database. Often, performance data will need to be derived or extracted. For example, performance data might be contained in compliance reports (regulatory reports, IRS 990 filings, final grant reports). Sometimes information is in other systems—project management systems, accounting systems, donor management systems, or case management systems.

Frequently, no data may be available at all for certain performance measures. This is not a dead end. In these cases, the best way to proceed is to talk to the process owner. Remember, each of the performance measures you've chosen is the result of some process (method, policy, or program) going on in the organization. Somewhere, somehow, someone (or some group) is responsible for that method, policy, or process. The process owner is the person, team, or program that is responsible for producing the outcome. (It will also be helpful, for the sake of convenience, to give a process name to the actions the process owner undertakes to achieve the outcomes you are measuring.) Odds are at least enough information is floating around in that person's head to set a baseline. One common mistake that many nonprofits make is to "give up" and not collect vital performance data because either it is too hard to collect or no mechanisms are in place to track it. As the Nature Conservancy "bucks-and-acres" example illustrates: collecting performance measures because they are easy to track can sometimes lead to measuring things that don't matter. So avoid the temptation to eliminate a measure just because it's difficult to track.

✔ **TASK:** *Collect Baseline Data*

Use Worksheet 8: Internal Data Collection, page 46, for tracking internal performance measures and benchmarks by outcome. The sample on page 45 provides an example of a completed worksheet.

[15] David Osborne and Ted Gaebler, *Reinventing Government: How the Entrepreneurial Spirit Is Transforming the Public Sector* (New York: Penguin Group, 1993), 147.

SAMPLE

Internal Data Collection Worksheet

Internal Data	
Critical to Quality (CTQ) Outcome: Improve cost-effectiveness and quality of business tools	
Process Name: Software purchasing	
Process Description: The process we go through to acquire software for the organization's computers. Includes researching, identifying, costing, and procuring software.	
Process Type (method/policy/program): Method	**Interrelated Processes:** Informal technology; data management
Process Lifecycle (MM/YY–MM/YY): Annual (01/04–12/04)	**Other:** Previously this was not a formal process at this organization; this is the first year it is being managed

Process Management	Process Financials
Best Practice Owner: Bill Jenson	**Annual Process Budget ($):** 10,000
Contact Information: bjenson@organization.org	**Highest Cost Item:** Accounting software
Reports to: Janice Weatherby	**Amount of Highest Cost ($):** 6,000

Performance Measures	
Performance Measure 1 Name: Cost of software	**Internal Baseline:** $10,000
Measure Type (%, #, $, Y/N): $	**Measure Period (MM/YY–MM/YY):** 01/04–12/04
Performance Measure 2 Name: User satisfaction	**Internal Baseline:** 4 or higher on 1–5 scale
Measure Type (%, #, $, Y/N): #	**Measure Period (MM/YY–MM/YY):** 01/04–12/04
Performance Measure 3 Name: n/a	**Internal Baseline:**
Measure Type (%, #, $, Y/N):	**Measure Period (MM/YY–MM/YY):**

Worksheet 8: Internal Data Collection

Instructions: Choose a CTQ outcome that you will be benchmarking. Then give a name ("process name") to the practice your organization uses to accomplish that outcome. Record your organization's current performance data below.

Internal Data

Critical to Quality (CTQ) Outcome:

Process Name:

Process Description:

Process Type (method/policy/program):	Interrelated Processes:
Process Lifecycle (MM/YY–MM/YY):	Other:

Process Management	Process Financials
Best Practice Owner:	Annual Process Budget ($):
Contact Information:	Highest Cost Item:
Reports to:	Amount of Highest Cost ($):

Performance Measures	
Performance Measure 1 Name:	Internal Baseline:
Measure Type (%, #, $, Y/N):	Measure Period (MM/YY–MM/YY):
Performance Measure 2 Name:	Internal Baseline:
Measure Type (%, #, $, Y/N):	Measure Period (MM/YY–MM/YY):
Performance Measure 3 Name:	Internal Baseline:
Measure Type (%, #, $, Y/N):	Measure Period (MM/YY–MM/YY):

Step 3C: Set Internal Benchmarks for Your Measures

Benchmarks can be thought of as guideposts that help you determine progress toward success. Absent a benchmark, a performance measure is relatively meaningless. Imagine, for example, the meaning of a baseball player's earned run average (ERA) without a benchmark. Everyone agrees Nolan Ryan was a great pitcher. His career ERA was 3.19.[16] Was that a good ERA? Should other pitchers use Ryan's ERA as a benchmark for a career ERA? The benchmark sets that parameter and allows you to proceed in your quest for best practices.

Nonprofit managers often use the term "benchmark" to mean many different things: performance measures, results, goals, or best practices. Some organizations seek to identify benchmarks as ends unto themselves. These can be helpful guideposts, but they are more useful if the underlying best practices that drove the results are also discovered. For example, assume a national nonprofit organization was looking to improve its employee retention. The organization decided that the measure of employee turnover rate (percent of employees that exit the organization on an annual basis) was a sufficient indicator of that outcome. It then surveyed one hundred affiliates and identified that the average employee turnover rate was 22 percent. In an effort to raise the bar, the organization set the benchmark for this measure at 10 percent. In other words, the goal for all affiliates was to lower their employee turnover rates to 10 percent or less.

The promulgation of the benchmark itself had great utility for the organization. Affiliates knew where they stood, managers were clear on what was an "acceptable" employee turnover rate, and outliers could be identified (say, the Sacramento affiliate had 60 percent turnover and the Chicago affiliate had 3 percent turnover). But the true power of the benchmark—and the ultimate benefit to benchmarking—is to help you identify a best practice. While it is useful to know that Chicago had an employee turnover rate of 3 percent, what the organization really should want to know is *why* it was 3 percent. What innovative methods, policies, or programs caused the Chicago chapter to retain so many employees?

For the purposes of this book, *benchmark* is the desired "stretch" performance goal assigned to a particular measure. That benchmark can be derived from your own historical performance (internal) or from your peers (external). A benchmark for a performance measure is like a budget. Accountants determine a "budget" in their accounting systems to denote the desired level of expenditure for particular items. Later, they compare the budgeted amount to the actual expenditures. Similarly, your benchmarking team will set a "budget" level of performance for each measure to denote the desired level of achievement. You can then compare the budget, or benchmark, level with the actual level of success or progress your organization experienced.

---

[16] Baseball-reference.com. http://www.baseball-reference.com/r/ryanno01.shtml.

Here are a few examples:

Performance Measure	Internal Benchmark	Actual Result
Client satisfaction rate	90%	66%
Housing units financed	100/month	145/month
Job placement	100%	88%
Earned income	$100,000/quarter	$150,000/quarter
Self-esteem growth	8 or higher (on 1–10 scale)	9.5

The Jumpstart Benchmarking Initiative sample, page 49, is an actual page from the benchmarking initiative of Jumpstart, an early childhood education program. In this case, Jumpstart uses the term "goal" to refer to the benchmark and "stretch" to denote an even higher level of desired performance. You can see that Jumpstart uses its performance measures to push toward improvement.

Benchmarks can be reported in a variety of ways. The Benchmarking Report sample, below, is an actual report from a nonprofit benchmarking system, listing the outcome, the measure, and the actual versus benchmark performance.

Q SAMPLE

Benchmarking Report

Key Outcomes	Actual	Benchmark	Progress Toward Benchmark	Momentum
Develop Innovative School Model				
# of new schools that obtain state sanctioned status for new design	18	22	8 — 22	−
# of new schools that report data on new school design	30	55	22 — 55	↓

Source: Mission Measurement (www.missionmeasurement.com)

⌕ SAMPLE

Jumpstart Benchmarking Initiative*

		Goal	Stretch	Month: April
Executive	GROWTH. Progress of the site growth toward long-term goals. Goal: 100 new Corps member (CM) slots at corporate sites; 200 New CM slots at affiliate sites Stretch: 120 new CM slots at corporate sites; 380 New CM slots at affiliate sites	420 new CM slots	500 new CM slots	Contemplates new CMs for FY02 and, as such, is still in progress. However, at least 8 new sites are now certain to be added in FY02, yielding 320 new CMs.
Organizational Development	VACANCY RATE. Percentage of Corps support positions that are unfilled.	20%	10%	National 1% NY 2% Boston .5% NH 0% DC 0%
Program: Service to Children	SESSION QUALITY. Average rating for the 8 Jumpstart session quality indicators in monitoring visits. Fall Spring Impact on children. Change in skill levels of children participating in Jumpstart. Fall/Spring show statistically significant gains in:	3.0 4.0 50% of the outcomes	3.5 4.5 70% of the outcomes	3.19 Awaiting Spring Is calculated over summer
Program Corps Members	CM RETENTION. Number of Corps members enrolled throughout the year, encompassing recruitment, retention, and graduation. 300-hour model 600-hour model 900-hour model	80% 70% 70%	85%+ 80%+ 75%+	57% 59% 79%
Development	REVENUE. Percentage of budget raised to quarterly fundraising benchmarks and year end total.	100%	110%	We have raised 70.1% of our year-end goal or 100% of the Scorecard's quarterly benchmark.
Finance	BUDGET. Percent of budget to expenditures, relative to enrollment.	2.1–5% under budget	0–2% under budget	-15%

* Allen Grossman and Arthur McCaffrey, "Jumpstart," *Harvard Business School Case Study 9-301-037*. Copyright © 2001 by the Presidents and Fellows of Harvard College.

✔ **TASK:** *Set an Internal Benchmark for Each of Your Measures*

Ask your benchmarking team to decide on an internal benchmark, or "target," you'd like to hit for each of your organization's performance measures. Use the internal data you collected to help set a baseline for each benchmark. Then use Worksheet 9: Set Benchmarks to record your benchmarks and to summarize your benchmarking process thus far.

Worksheet 9: Set Benchmarks

Fill in your CTQ outcomes, identified in Worksheet 5, along the left hand side. Fill in your performance measures, identified in Worksheet 6, in the second column. In the third column, fill in the baseline for that performance measure (identified in Worksheet 8). Finally, note the benchmark goals for each performance measure in the far right column.

CTQ Outcome	Performance Measure	Baseline	Benchmark

Summary

You have come a long way. After figuring out what your organization must do to succeed, you determined some ways of measuring your work—the performance measurements set in Chapter 2. In this chapter, you tested those measurements using SMART criteria: a performance measure should be specific, measurable, accountable, results-oriented, and time-bound.

Having decided what to measure, you set a baseline (or your organization's actual performance level) based on data available to you. Finally, with baselines set, you established internal benchmarks, or performance targets, that will help you determine your organization's progress.

Setting internal benchmarks is fine but, ultimately, not helpful unless you have ways to reach those benchmarks. The next chapter will help you gather data and find best practices to help your organization meet its performance goals.

Performance measurement can benefit your organization in many ways

In a United Way survey, respondents agreed that implementing measurement was helpful in many different ways:

- 88 percent said it helped to communicate program results
- 88 percent said it focused staff effort on common goals and purposes
- 86 percent said it clarified the purpose of the program
- 83 percent said it helped them successfully compete for resources/funding

* Source: *Agency Experiences with Outcome Measurement*, United Way of America, Item Number 0196, January 2000, p. 5.

CHAPTER 4

Learn What Works

In 1996, the organizers of the United Nation's Habitat II City Summit Conference hatched a novel idea. Why not build on the success of the conference by creating a database of innovative social programs from around the world and sharing them online? In partnership with the Together Foundation, the UN launched the UN Habitat Best Practices Database. The online database included over 1,600 proven solutions from more than 140 countries.

While the stories are interesting and the prospect of having all the answers in one place is enticing, the reality is that a catalog of best practices is of limited use. An organization can't just apply someone else's best practice without first going through the hard work of figuring out what outcomes and performance measures apply to its particular situation. At that point, the organization can actively seek best practices based on its understanding of what other organizations did that made them better at certain benchmarks. In other words, copying someone else's "best practice" (based on some outsider's criteria) is of limited utility if you have not figured out what you need help on and sought relevant improvements.

Fortunately, if you've worked your way to this step, you're ready to seek out best practices. You've listed the ultimate impact you want to improve within your organization (impact goals), identified the outcomes that matter most to those goals (CTQ outcomes), and identified performance measures you can use to measure the success in achieving an outcome. You've also figured out how well your organization is performing (set a baseline) and how much you hope to improve (set an internal benchmark).

You have identified your outcomes, found the right performance measures, set baselines, and established benchmarks for your organization. Now you can begin to gather data and tease out best practices that will help you improve your performance. In Step 4, you will

- Select benchmarking partners
- Collect data
- Analyze performance gaps
- Identify best practices

Now you need to look outside your organization. You have to identify more successful and efficient means of achieving a particular outcome your organization desires. These successful innovations, methods, or techniques of top-performing organizations are best practices. When you find organizations that you think do something you do, but do it better, you can try to link up with them so you can learn from them—to become benchmarking partners.

Step 4A: Select Benchmarking Partners

Your job in this step is to be a sleuth: You will investigate the mystery of why one organization, department, or affiliate has experienced dramatically higher performance than yours. Your mission is to "tease out" the best practices or underlying innovations that explain superior results. A best practice may be subtle or glaringly obvious.

Regardless of how you conduct your search for best practices, you must first identify appropriate *benchmarking partners*. A benchmarking partner can be another department, function, or person within your own organization, or it can be another nonprofit, a company, or a government agency.

Choosing the right benchmarking partners

Identifying best practices in peer organizations (or even in other departments within your organization) can be challenging. With so many different potential partners, you will need to narrow the field. Figure 2, below, illustrates different types of commonalities between you and best practice organizations (or departments). Remember, it is not necessary for a best practice to come from within your organization, or even from another nonprofit. Use the chart in Figure 2 to help you identify comparable elements between you and a potential partner. For each combination, the chart will tell you whether or not a partner with those characteristics is likely to yield an applicable best practice.

Figure 2. Benchmarking Partner Assessment Chart

If your partner has:	Different success equation	Different performance measures	Different outcomes
Similar success equation		Benchmarking is possible	Benchmarking is possible
Similar performance measures	Benchmarking not applicable		Benchmarking not applicable
Similar outcomes	Benchmarking is applicable	Benchmarking is possible	

Here are two illustrations to show how this plays out.

Example 1: *Different Success Equations.* Take two welfare-to-work organizations, one run by the state of Wisconsin, the other run by the state of Florida. Both are trying to reduce the number of people on state welfare rolls (same ultimate impact). The Wisconsin program's success equation rests on a "work first" strategy: in other words, it believes that the best way to relieve the swelling welfare rolls is to get people into any job, regardless of quality or sustainability. Once people are working, the theory goes, they will pick up basic skills and become inherently more employable. Therefore, Wisconsin's outcomes relate to the volume of recipients being placed in jobs. The Florida program has quite a different definition of success: it is built on the premise of "graduating" people from welfare into sustainable, long-term jobs. Florida's outcomes focus more on salary per recipient, recidivism rates, and sustainability of employment.

Analysis: Both Wisconsin and Florida are trying to achieve similar programmatic impacts (reducing dependency on state welfare rolls). However, since they have diverging approaches to what "success" means, and therefore fundamentally different outcomes, benchmarking will be less likely to yield best practices.

Example 2: *Similar Outcomes.* A small battered-women's shelter has struggled constantly with turnover in its senior ranks—going through three executive directors in two years. So the organization set as a goal to improve job retention of its key employees. The organization's outcomes included improved morale, increased advancement opportunities, and more employee benefits. The shelter then researched potential benchmark partners and found a Fortune 500 pharmaceutical firm and a local restaurant. Both companies were very different in size and mission from the nonprofit organization. However, all three were focused on a similar set of outcomes related to improving retention of key personnel. The nonprofit was able to compare retention rates and learn some innovative practices at each of the benchmarking partners that it never would have thought of on its own.

Analysis: Even though these organizations were all very different—a small shelter, a pharmaceutical company, and a restaurant—benchmarking was possible because they were trying to solve the same problem. Similar outcomes always allow for benchmarking.

Where to find best practices

You can learn from a virtually unlimited number of organizations: there are millions of possible nonprofit groups, public sector agencies, and some businesses. And that's just in the United States! Even international benchmarking has become more in vogue over the past five years.

The most popular ways to research and identify best practices are also the most obvious ones:

- Internal resources (contacts, files, library)
- Conferences
- Trade associations
- Internet
- Trade magazines
- Awards programs
- Foundations
- Consultants
- Constituents
- Academics
- Case studies

What can you learn from these examples? In the first example, both organizations had similar long-term impacts—but their different theories about how to achieve that impact made them incompatible as benchmarking partners. In the second example, three organizations that appeared to be very different actually shared a common outcome, making them compatible. The lesson here is to be sure you're looking for the right items to compare; don't be misled by outward similarities. (Of course, Florida and Wisconsin can still learn from each other by comparing and challenging their different approaches to welfare reform—but that is a goal outside of the capacities of benchmarking.)

What you can learn from unusual partners

Organizations can learn a tremendous amount from atypical benchmarking partners. While dissimilar organizations often have very different networks, experiences, and training, they may face similar problems with regard to achieving the same types of outcomes or streamlining the same types of practices. Here are a few good examples:

Xerox and L. L. Bean: A Xerox logistics team identified the order processing and fulfillment operation at L. L. Bean as a benchmarking partner to help improve its warehousing productivity because of Bean's superior performance with a similar process. [Source: Robert C. Camp, *Benchmarking: The Search for Industry Best Practices That Lead to Superior Performance* (Milwaukee, WI: ASQC Quality Press, 1989), 41.]

Dalbar Financial Services and the Social Security Administration: Dalbar, America's biggest financial news publisher, studied the way the Social Security Administration (SSA) handled 64 million calls each year on its toll-free number in order to benchmark 800-number customer service standards. (And in order to get so good, the SSA studied American Express, Saturn Corporation, AT&T, and the GE Answer Center.) [Source: Al Gore, *Common Sense Government: Works Better and Costs Less* (New York: Random House, 1995), 77–78.]

Boston Ballet and Au Bon Pain: The Boston Ballet, while nationally acclaimed for its artistic quality, felt it wasn't receiving the attention it deserved. Led by the ballet's board chair, the organization looked at organizations that enjoyed popular support. These included other ballet companies, the Boston Museum of Science (which had improved its image in recent years), and Au Bon Pain (a fast-growing Boston food chain with a reputation for good customer service). [Source: Christine W. Letts, William P. Ryan, and Allen Grossman, *High Performance Nonprofit Organizations: Managing Upstream for Greater Impact* (New York: John Wiley & Sons, 1999), 94.]

General Mills and NASCAR: As the economy struggled in 2002 and 2003, General Mills looked for ways to drastically cut costs from its manufacturing lines. It studied the way a NASCAR pit crew was able to work with blinding speed simply through better organization. This inspired General Mills to cut the time it took workers to change a production line from one Betty Crocker product to another (from more than four hours to just twelve minutes). [Source: Pallavi Gogoi, "Thinking Outside the Cereal Box," *BusinessWeek* (July 28, 2003), http://www.businessweek.com/magazine/content/03_32/b3845089_mz017.htm]

TASK: *Identify Potential Benchmarking Partners* ✔

Use Worksheet 10: Brainstorm Potential Benchmarking Partners to brainstorm and list potential benchmarking partners. Choose partners who are driving at the same critical to quality outcome that you are, but seem to be doing better at it. You will be brainstorming at this point—trying to figure out, by virtue of reputation or some other information, organizations with whom you might compare yourself around some critical to quality outcome. Your benchmarking team members should come up with the initial list of potential partners based on their industry experience. Then expand your inquiry to board members, service providers, funders, and colleagues.

Worksheet 10: Brainstorm Potential Benchmarking Partners

Below, list one of your CTQ outcomes from Worksheet 9. Then brainstorm organizations that you think do a better job on this outcome.

CTQ Outcome: _____

Partner Name	Contact Info (e-mail, phone)	Why you think they're a good potential partner

Step 4B: Collect Data

After you've identified benchmarking partners, you can begin collecting information about potential best practices. There are two ways to do this—informally and formally. Informal collection is less rigorous, can happen faster, and is often well suited to many goals. Formal data collection is more time-consuming but may yield richer results.

Informal data collection

Informal data collection is a "gut-feel" approach to identifying best practices. You "eyeball" the performance of a potential partner without formally collecting and comparing much performance data. A lot can be learned from reading about your partner or informally speaking with another business process owner.

Case in point: A small nonprofit organization based in Chicago wanted to improve its fundraising. One of its critical to quality outcomes was "increasing the number of leads generated through its web site." A quick keyword search on Google revealed that the nonprofit's web site was not ranked highly in the search results. In fact, it didn't show up until the sixth page of results! At a reception, the executive director of that organization bumped into an old friend who ran the marketing department at a local commodities trading firm. As they chatted about her work, she told him that she was in charge of generating leads for her company. She explained that instead of spending a lot of money on direct mail or advertising to get hits on her company's web site, she had researched and hired a local search engine optimization expert for a small amount of money. After doing so, her company was able to achieve page one rankings in several major search engines, including Google. The executive director returned home that evening, plugged in a keyword for his friend's company, and, bingo, found that it was indeed the top search result on Google. He got the name of the search optimization consultant and applied the best practice to his organization.

Always try informal data collection first. It's quick, easy, and cost free. Informal data collection usually involves networking and investigating publicly available data sources. If this approach doesn't pan out for you, you can always move on to formal benchmarking.

Formal data collection

Formal data collection employs the same techniques as informal data collection but in a more scientific and systematic manner. Formal benchmarking uses a benchmarking survey or questionnaire to gather performance data from benchmarking partners. You can collect data via site visits or phone interviews. You can also collect data through secondary sources. (Worksheet 11: Benchmarking Partner Performance Data, page 62, gives you space to collect this data.)

The question often arises, Why would someone share this proprietary information with me? You might be surprised. The benchmarking partnership is usually bilateral, meaning you will also share your organization's data with your partner. Also, organization leaders love to talk about their organization's work, and they are often honored that you consider their practice or innovation worthy of replication. Last, some organizations—for-profit and nonprofit—generally believe that they have a duty to help improve the nonprofit sector. By sharing their best practices with you, they are helping to elevate the level of service to the community, and that is generally perceived as a badge of good corporate citizenship.

During site visits or while conducting secondary research, make sure you collect as much "context" information as possible in addition to the data points. Why? In your analysis you will need to determine whether or not the identified practice is one that can be replicated. In order to do so, you will need to know as much as you can about what explains the partner's superior performance. Was it due to an innovation? Or was it due to a unique circumstance (charismatic leader, "creaming" results, unusual economic factors)? Does this organization have a track record of success, or is this an overnight sensation? How much historical data is available on the best practice? (See Step 4D: Identify Best Practices, page 68, for more on analyzing the context.)

Site visits can be useful in more than one way. First, interviewing prospective benchmarking partners allows you to take a look "under the hood" of the organization you are studying, to see its practices firsthand. Second, site visits build relationships that can endure and turn into collaborations, sponsorships, and other useful alliances. The learning phase of benchmarking requires a close working relationship with your benchmarking partners, and meeting them in person is one way to deepen that rapport.

TASK: *Collect Performance Data* ✔

Worksheet 11: Benchmarking Partner Performance Data, page 62, provides a form for formal data collection. Use a separate worksheet for each benchmarking partner. The sample data collection forms, pages 60–61, show information for leads generated on a web site, the example discussed on page 58. Here you can see the relatively low performance levels of the inquiring organization as compared to those of its benchmarking partner organization.

🔍 SAMPLE

Benchmarking Performance Data, 1

Benchmarking Partner Name: *Our Organization*	
Critical to Quality (CTQ) Outcome: Increase number of donor leads through web site. The goal is to improve the number of the potential donors visiting our web site and at the same time reduce the amount of money we are spending on marketing.	
Process Name: Online lead generation (donors)	
Process Description: The process we go through to register, rank, and promote traffic to our organization's web site in order to acquire leads (i.e. potential donors)	
Beneficiaries: Development, marketing	
Process Type (method/policy/program): Method	**Interrelated Processes:** Information technology; direct marketing, donor development
Process Lifecycle (MM/YY–MM/YY): Monthly (01/04-02/04)	**Other:** Used to be part of IT, now is a marketing function

Process Management	**Process Financials**
Best Practice Owner: Mary Jane Olmstead	**Annual Process Budget ($):** 7,500
Contact Information: molmstead@organization.org	**Highest Cost Item:** Direct mail
Reports to: Lester Morrison	**Amount of Highest Cost ($):** 5,000

Performance Measures	
Performance Measure 1 Name: Monthly web site traffic	**Internal Baseline:** 2000 unique visitors
Measure Type (%, #, $, Y/N): #	**Measure Period (MM/YY–MM/YY):** 01/04–02/04
Performance Measure 2 Name: Search engine ranking (Google)	**Internal Baseline:** First page result
Measure Type (%, #, $, Y/N): #	**Measure Period (MM/YY–MM/YY):** 01/04–02/04
Performance Measure 3 Name: Cost per lead	**Internal Baseline:** $50
Measure Type (%, #, $, Y/N): $	**Measure Period (MM/YY–MM/YY):** 01/04–02/04

SAMPLE

Benchmarking Performance Data, 2

Benchmarking Partner Name: *XYZ*	
Critical to Quality (CTQ) Outcome: Increase sales leads through web site. Improve traffic to web site and number of potential customers who convert to leads.	
Process Name: Online lead generation (customers)	
Process Description: The process we go through to register, rank, and promote traffic to our organization's web site in order to acquire leads (i.e. potential customers)	
Beneficiaries: Sales, marketing	
Process Type (method/policy/program): Method	**Interrelated Processes:** Information technology; direct marketing, sales
Process Lifecycle (MM/YY–MM/YY): Monthly (01/04-02/04)	**Other:** n/a
Process Management	**Process Financials**
Best Practice Owner: Christina Stevenson	**Annual Process Budget ($):** 30,000
Contact Information: cstevenson@company.com	**Highest Cost Item:** Banner ads
Reports to: Morris Millerman	**Amount of Highest Cost ($):** 3,000
Performance Measures	
Performance Measure 1 Name: Monthly web site traffic	**Benchmark:** 50,000 unique visitors
Measure Type (%, #, $, Y/N): #	**Measure Period (MM/YY–MM/YY):** 01/04–02/04
Performance Measure 2 Name: Search engine ranking (Google)	**Benchmark:** First page result
Measure Type (%, #, $, Y/N): #	**Measure Period (MM/YY–MM/YY):** 01/04–02/04
Performance Measure 3 Name: Cost per lead	**Benchmark:** $4
Measure Type (%, #, $, Y/N): $	**Measure Period (MM/YY–MM/YY):** 01/04–02/04

Worksheet 11: Benchmarking Partner Performance Data

Instructions: Choose a CTQ outcome that you will be benchmarking. Then, describe the process your benchmarking partner uses to accomplish that outcome. Fill in the rest of the worksheet as appropriate, describing who benefits from the process, its budget, and so forth.

Benchmarking Partner Name:

Critical to Quality (CTQ) Outcome:

Process Name:

Process Description:

Beneficiaries:

Process Type (method/policy/program):	Interrelated Processes:
Process Lifecycle (MM/YY–MM/YY):	Other:

Process Management	Process Financials
Best Practice Owner:	Annual Process Budget ($):
Contact Information:	Highest Cost Item:
Reports to:	Amount of Highest Cost ($):

Performance Measures	
Performance Measure 1 Name:	Benchmark:
Measure Type (%, #, $, Y/N): #	Measure Period (MM/YY–MM/YY):
Performance Measure 2 Name:	Benchmark:
Measure Type (%, #, $, Y/N):	Measure Period (MM/YY–MM/YY):
Performance Measure 3 Name:	Benchmark:
Measure Type (%, #, $, Y/N):	Measure Period (MM/YY–MM/YY):

Step 4C: Analyze Performance Gaps

Now it is time to evaluate the data you've collected from your benchmarking partners. For this task, you will compare your organization's baseline results to the performance data that you collected from benchmarking partners (either informally or formally). The process of analyzing the performance differential between your organization and a best practice candidate is referred to as *gap analysis*. The gap itself is called a *performance margin*. Gap analysis can be used to determine best practices in two ways:

1. **Qualitative gap analysis (intuitive)**

   This analysis involves identifying an innovative or successful practice regardless of measures. Some practices may be so superior that they are quite obviously best practices. In other cases, superiority may be evidenced by success with funders or strong demand among constituents—something researchers refer to as "marketplace superiority."[17] The fact that quantitative gap analysis cannot be performed should not deter you from recognizing a best practice when you see one. The evidence in qualitative gap analysis is principally anecdotal, descriptive analysis (such as low-cost donor acquisition through the use of the Internet or high client output as a result of team training).

2. **Quantitative gap analysis (statistical)**

   This analysis compares the relative performance of multiple organizations against common measures. Quantitative gap analysis identifies the performance margin between your organization and the best in class. Identifying a performance gap will prompt your team to ask why, which will reveal a best practice or other underlying explanation. The evidence in this type of analysis is principally numbers-based (such as $10 per donor acquired or 500 people served per month).

Qualitative gap analysis

Qualitative gap analysis is a fancy term for "eyeballing." Many partner organizations have scant performance data available. This means you may need to eyeball the gap between your organization and a possible high performer. The trick to qualitative analysis is to be as rigorous as possible, even without data. You're trying to analyze the best practice based on attributes, characteristics, strategies, and practices, rather than measures.

Consider an example: the Radio Center for People with Disabilities (RCPD), a tiny training and job placement facility based in Chicago. A few years ago, RCPD was seeking to improve its relationships with corporate partners. Through research on the

---

[17] Robert C. Camp, *Benchmarking: The Search for Industry Best Practices That Lead to Superior Performance* (Milwaukee, WI: ASQC Quality Press, 1989), 127.

web, networking, and a few good books, the organization identified several examples of nonprofits that had established successful relationships with corporate partners:

Share Our Strength (SOS) and American Express. Share Our Strength (SOS), a leading antihunger organization, partnered with American Express in 1993 to create the "Charge for Hunger" program. Through the program, SOS raised $21 million to distribute to antihunger organizations throughout the United States.

KaBOOM! and Home Depot. The home-improvement giant provided volunteers and donated supplies and cash to KaBOOM!, a nonprofit that builds playgrounds in inner cities.

Techsoup and Microsoft. Microsoft provided Techsoup, a web portal designed to help nonprofits learn about technology, with millions of dollars of free software each year. Techsoup resold the software to nonprofits for a small fee and generated revenues from the sales to fund its education and training programs.

In each of these cases, not enough data was available about the terms of the arrangements, the net benefits each accrued to the nonprofit, or the leverage for additional fundraising made possible by these partnerships. But RCPD made a qualitative judgment that these partnerships appeared to be a valuable mechanism for securing corporate support. RCPD's qualitative gap analysis can be seen in the sample below.

Q SAMPLE

Radio Center for People with Disabilities Qualitative Gap Analysis

Process Name: *Partner development with corporate sponsors*

CTQ Outcome	Our Organization	Benchmark Partner 1	Benchmark Partner 2
Corporate Sponsors	None	Some $ raised	Lots of $ raised
$ Raised	$ Thousands	$ Tens of thousands	$ Millions
Public Visibility	Medium	High	High

In addition, the research conducted during qualitative gap analysis led RCPD to draw conclusions about some common best practice attributes and characteristics of a successful partnership. Here's what RCPD found:

- In each case, there was a synergy between needs and assets. The nonprofit's assets—reach, brand, and so forth—were congruent with something the corporation valued.

- In each case, the two organizations had a good cultural fit. They shared similar principles and their representatives got along well together.

- In each case, there was a "deal champion." Someone inside the corporate partner cared enough about the deal to push through the obstacles and make it happen.

Using these best practice lessons, RCPD went on to build successful partnerships with several corporate partners: iRobot Corporation, Clear Channel Communications, Radio & Records Magazine, and Arbitron.

Experienced benchmarkers suggest analyzing best practices on a qualitative basis before doing quantitative analysis. Why? You first have to make a "gut" judgment about a potential best practice (a qualitative step) in order to deem it worthy of collecting performance data and analyzing it more closely (a quantitative step). Documenting that judgment is really what quantitative analysis is all about.

Quantitative gap analysis

The purpose of gap analysis is to identify measurable opportunities for performance improvement within your organization's current processes. This comparison can help your team determine what level of improvement is possible. The more significant the difference between your performance and the best practice, the more opportunity there is to improve. The performance margin can be positive or negative. A positive performance margin implies that you are performing at levels above your external best practice candidates. A negative performance margin implies that the best practices you have selected are performing at levels superior to your organization.

Performance margins are identified by laying out the comparative measures for a particular practice in a chart and tabulating the differential in the right-most column. The Quantitative Gap Analysis sample, page 66, illustrates how quantitative gap analysis can be applied.

In the sample below, the performance margin is determined by the positive or negative directional difference between the measures. For example, the best practice candidate demonstrated a 43 percent higher level of client satisfaction. Additional best practice candidates can be added and a gap between the baseline and the industry average can be determined. The employee turnover measure shows a positive gap: the baseline organization is performing above the proposed best practice. In some cases, this may indeed be true and validates that your organization's current approach is best in class. In other cases, one measure might not tell the whole story and additional measures may be required.

SAMPLE

Quantitative Gap Analysis

Performance Measure	Our Baseline	Partner's Benchmark	Gap (Performance Margin)
Client satisfaction rate	55%	98%	-43%
Housing units financed	100/month	255/month	-155/month
Job placement	70%	88%	-18%
Earned income	$100,000/quarter	$750,000/quarter	-$650,000/quarter
Employee turnover	10%	15%	+5%

Your first instinct may be to cast off extreme variances as outliers. Don't. Oftentimes in benchmarking—particularly in the nonprofit world where performance has not been compared systematically—you will find extraordinary gaps.

✔ **TASK:** *Perform Gap Analysis*

Use Worksheet 12: Gap Analysis, page 67, to practice performing qualitative and quantitative gap analysis with your benchmarking team.

Worksheet 12: Gap Analysis

Fill out this worksheet using the performance data you gathered both internally and from benchmarking partners.

A. Qualitative Gap Analysis

Use Part A, Qualitative Gap Analysis, if your benchmarking partner has little performance data available. Once the table is filled in, you will "eyeball" a possible high performer.

Process Name: _____

CTQ Outcome	Our Organization	Benchmarking Partner Name:	Benchmarking Partner Name:

B. Quantitative Gap Analysis

Fill in the baseline and partner benchmarks from the data collection worksheets you filled out in Steps 3B and 4B. Calculate the difference between the baseline and each partner's benchmark to fill in the Gap columns.

Performance Measure	Baseline	Partner 1's Benchmark Name:	Gap (+/-)	Partner 2's Benchmark Name:	Gap (+/-)

Step 4D: Identify Best Practices

Once you have identified the performance margin (the gap) between your baseline and the best practice candidates, the next task is to ask why. What accounts for this significant difference in performance? Specifically, you are looking to identify the underlying process innovations (unique methods, programs, or policies) that are responsible for the extraordinary results. These underlying factors are the golden nuggets: the best practices.

In asking why, be sure to consider whether the process innovation is really a best practice or just a red herring. A red herring means that the reasons for the partner's breakthrough performance might have nothing to do with innovation whatsoever. Here are a few classic examples:

> **Red Herring 1:** *Charismatic Leader.* Consider the case of a venerated nonprofit organization in Cleveland. This organization had a renowned executive director, beloved by the community, polished in his style, and networked throughout the city from two decades of civic engagement. He was a first-rate fundraiser. Under his leadership, the organization raised more funds, on fewer dollars spent, than any other organization in its class. Hands down. But it wasn't a replicable best practice. Because even though the organization had similar performance measures and outcomes to another organization seeking to maximize the same process, this charismatic leader was so unique that the "best practice" was not repeatable.

> **Red Herring 2:** *Creaming.* The term "creaming" refers to skimming off, or separating, the best of something from the mass. A local high school introduced a new arts program to expose students to careers in the arts and humanities. By tracking the careers of early program participants, the staff were able to boast breakthrough results: 80 percent wound up in arts-related careers. Peer organizations began to look at these results as an industry benchmark for arts-education programs. Upon closer examination, it turned out that the school's arts program only admitted students with a demonstrated interest or talent in the arts. It is likely that most of the program participants would have gone into arts careers anyway.

> **Red Herring 3:** *Intervening Variables.* Consider the example of a program that aims to connect unemployed residents in South Chicago, a disadvantaged neighborhood, to employment opportunities. An affiliated program in Seattle conducted a benchmarking project and found that the South Chicago branch had breakthrough results in 2003. It placed 67 percent of its participants into jobs, while the Seattle baseline placed 23 percent. Upon further investigation, Seattle found out that what drove the South Chicago results wasn't really a best practice. A new factory, which happened to open in 2003 near South Chicago, had hired many neighborhood residents, and this explained the dramatic increase in performance.

After checking for red herrings, it's time to go deeper into why. To guide your investigation, ask these questions of each best practice candidate. If you can answer them compellingly, you've probably got a best practice:

- Is there a proven track record of success?
- Are the results sustainable?
- Can the idea be replicated?
- Is it cost-effective?
- Does it matter to the mission?

Best practices usually challenge the status quo. Therefore, the burden of proof will always fall to the benchmarking team to demonstrate that a proposed best practice is truly superior to the current method, program, or policy. Take this task seriously. In order to inspire your organization to improve, you will need to have your facts straight and plenty of evidence to support your case for change.

TASK: *Identify a Best Practice*   ✔

Apply the questionnaire in Worksheet 13, page 70, to your best practice candidates.

The samples on pages 71–72 illustrate two best practices an organization identified while working with its national chapters on benchmarking.

What else can you learn?

Identifying best practices to improve performance is the primary objective in a benchmarking endeavor. But some extremely valuable secondary benefits and lessons also can be gleaned from gap analysis.

Learn what measures others are using
One benefit that can be captured from studying other organizations is learning how to improve your system of measures. For example, if your organization is trying to improve its donor relations, you may learn that a better measure of donor satisfaction is the number of donors that renew each year, rather than the number of new donors each year. Renewals actually have a better link to improving relations.

Learn the effectiveness of other theories of change
Even though an organization may have a different problem-solving approach, you may find that its theory of change is actually better. For example, a child-centered behavior modification program may discover that another organization that focuses on the entire family has better results. It may decide to modify its success equation accordingly.

Find new partners and allies
The most powerful benefits of benchmarking are sometimes the least obvious. For example, consider a homeless shelter and a drug rehabilitation program. These organizations have vastly different programs, processes, and measures. Yet through benchmarking, the homeless shelter might learn that the drug rehabilitation program is seeking to achieve the same programmatic outcome (graduating individuals into sustainable jobs). Even though these organizations have ostensibly nothing in common, they are attempting to solve the same problem, from different yet potentially complementary vantage points, and might find collaboration useful.

Worksheet 13: Best Practice Questionnaire

Ask your best practice candidates the following questions:

Name of organization where best practice occurred: _____

1. CTQ Outcome:

2. Performance Measure:

3. Internal Benchmark:

4. Best Practice:

5. Best Practice Owner (the person or department responsible for the best practice):

6. Why? What accounts for the difference?

7. Underlying process innovations (unique methods, programs, policies)?

8. Is there a track record of success in this process?

9. Are the results sustainable?

10. Can the idea be replicated?

11. Is it cost- and/or time-effective?

12. How does it help you achieve your mission?

Q SAMPLE

Best Practice Summary, 1

1. **CTQ Outcome:** Participation at board and committee meetings

2. **Performance Measure:** % attendance (excluding excused absences)

3. **Internal Benchmark:** 90 – 100%

4. **Best Practice:** 100%

5. **Best Practice Owner:** XYZ Chapter of the Heartland

6. **Why? What accounts for the difference?**
   - The board meets only three times a year.
   - New board members are told how important attendance is. It is an expectation of board members.
   - Board meetings are rotated among the three states.
   - They have a small board, reduced to 9 from 15 over the past few years. The 6 open positions will be filled strategically with people who are affluent, influential, and fill a geographic need.
   - If a board member can't travel to a meeting, they can participate by conference call.
   - The CEO meets with local board members when she travels to the various sites.
   - The CEO e-mails bi-monthly updates to the board so they can keep up to speed between meetings.

7. **Underlying process innovations (unique methods, programs, policies)?**
   Feedback from new board members indicated that they wanted more orientation because of the complexity of the organization's programs and because they only meet three times a year. A dinner with an experienced board member and the CEO is held before a new member's first board meeting. This helps with camaraderie and mentoring of the new member. The CEO calls new members after their first board meeting to see if they have any questions.

   There are three board committees that meet three times a year each. Committee reports are sent in advance, not given at board meetings, at the board's request. Board meetings only deal with issues requiring board input. This change received good feedback from the board.

8. **Do you have a track record of success in this process?**
   Attendance improved after the board was reduced from 15 to 9. Board engagement has been evolving positively since then.

9. **Are the results sustainable?** Yes.

10. **Can the idea be replicated?** Yes.

11. **Is it cost- and/or time-effective?** Yes.

12. **How does it help you achieve your mission? Why does it matter?**
    As the governing body of the organization, board engagement and participation is crucial.

⌕ SAMPLE

Best Practice Summary, 2

1. **CTQ Outcome:** Change in net assets ratio

2. **Performance Measure:** % change in net assets ratio FY2003 over FY2002

3. **Internal Benchmark:** A positive increase

4. **Best Practice:** 10.8%

5. **Best Practice Owner:** XYZ Chapter of the Southwest

6. **Why? What accounts for the significant difference?**
   This chapter is a growth and bottom-line-oriented organization. The larger it grows, the more important good financial management, cash management, better cash flow through quicker receivables collections becomes. Financials are closely monitored on a monthly basis. It responds quickly to variances.

7. **Underlying process innovations (unique methods, programs, policies)?**
   They used acquisition to expand their base and footprint, but managed their business to achieve surpluses at the same time.

8. **Do you have a track record of success in this process?**
   Yes, they haven't had a deficit in 18 years, even through years of growth.

9. **Are the results sustainable?** Yes.

10. **Can the idea be replicated?** Yes.

11. **Is it cost- and/or time-effective?** Yes, it would cost the organization too much not to do it.

12. **How does it help you achieve your mission? Why does it matter?**
    Yes, "No margin, no mission." Surpluses from operations are put back into services and include providing free and subsidized services, so achieving surpluses directly contributes to achieving the mission.

Summary

To identify best practices you must first choose the right benchmarking partners. By analyzing whether an organization has similar or different success equations, outcomes, and performance measures, you can cull potential partners from a near-endless list of possibilities.

Once you've determined whom to contact, you can start collecting data—either informally (identifying best practices without evaluating performance measures) or formally (through surveys, questionnaires, or interviews).

When evaluating the data you've collected from benchmarking partners, you can do either a quantitative gap analysis (statistical) or a qualitative gap analysis (intuitive). Both of these processes will uncover the performance differential between your organization and the best practice candidate. Once you have identified the performance difference between your baseline and the best practice candidates, you can start asking what processes the benchmarking partner uses that could be replicated to improve your organization's performance. The answer to this question is the best practice.

Chapter 5 will show you how to best implement the best practice you discovered in this chapter.

Implement Best Practices

Once you have conducted gap analysis, your team will have the opportunity to set new standards (reset benchmarks) for your organization. This is often more involved than simply copying a new process. Your benchmarking team must conduct a careful analysis of your organization's resources, structure, and culture. The best way to do this is through careful planning—and, usually, the creation of a formal plan.

Step 5A: Create an Implementation Plan

An implementation plan will identify the procedures that must be undertaken in order to import a best practice. There are usually three sections to the plan: goal setting, process planning, and rollout.

1. Set internal goals

Once you've identified a best practice, you then reset your internal benchmarks. For example, if in step 3C you set a benchmark of 50 percent seminar participation and you found out that the best practice was 85 percent, you would adjust your internal benchmark to 85 percent. In some cases, the best practice level of performance may not be appropriate for your organization—the time, resources, and expertise required to achieve the best practice goal are unrealistic. Instead, you should determine a reasonable level of performance for your organization and set the internal benchmark at that level.

Now that you have identified your outcomes, prioritized the processes you want to benchmark, defined the right measures, and identified best practices, you must consider how to "import" or apply these best practices to your own organization. In Step 5, you will

- Create an implementation plan
- Overcome staff resistance
- Create a staff communication plan
- Implement the best practice

2. Understand the process

Once the new benchmark is set, the next phase is process planning. This involves mapping out the best practice process and comparing it to your current process. The purpose of this is to figure out how to redesign the way you do things, change roles in the organization, or reallocate resources to be able to accomplish the new goals. Every outcome at a nonprofit organization has a process (method, program, or policy) or set of processes. The process has an owner: the person, team, or department that manages a particular set of activities. The benchmarking team will need to work with that process owner to set expectations about the levels of performance that are realistically achievable, the time frame within which performance can be improved, and the level of additional resources that may be required.

3. Plan for change

The third phase is rollout. This section should address the following questions: What needs to be accomplished within our organization to make the best practice happen? What's the time frame? Will new people need to be hired or jobs need to be cut? What cultural objections are anticipated? How will these be overcome? Who is going to be the process champion? What's the fallback plan? Who will monitor and report on the success of this new process? The benchmarking team should think carefully about these questions. Implementing change—even small changes—can take the organization in an entirely new direction, and the more scenarios you rehearse, the better you will be prepared.

 TASK: *Draft an Implementation Plan for a Best Practice*

Use Worksheet 14, page 79, to draft an implementation plan for each CTQ outcome you are benchmarking. Refer to Creating an Implementation Plan, page 77, for an example of one organization's implementation plan.

Q SAMPLE

Creating an Implementation Plan

Overview: *Recently, the executive committee of a foundation decided it wanted to benchmark and improve the foundation's grant evaluation process. The foundation had been doing virtually no post-grant evaluation, and the executive committee was feeling the heat from the board and donors to become more accountable. A benchmarking team was able to identify a best practice and began to shape the plan for implementation. The best practice was a new software product being used by another funder that helped the organization measure grant outcomes and track results. The process owner—the head of programs—was also the champion for this new best practice. But some of the program staff had been on the job for more than twenty years and were very reluctant to change. In addition, others were still uncomfortable using computers. Nevertheless, the executive committee persevered and decided to adopt the best practice. Here's how it worked through the phases of the implementation plan.*

Implementation Plan

1. **Internal goals.** The foundation currently evaluated 5 percent of its grants. After adopting the best practice, the executive committee set a new internal benchmark: 90 percent of all discretionary grants over $25,000 would have outcomes formally reported by the end of every grant cycle.

2. **Process redesign.** First, the process owner was identified. She was fully in support of adopting the best practice, so motivation was not an issue. Next, she was asked to map out the existing process in detail. Finally, the process owner superimposed the new process onto the current one, to identify issues or potential changes that would be necessary. (See the schematic on the next page.)

   However, internal discussions brought other staff issues to the surface. Most of the foundation's program officers had an established routine of receiving a proposal, preparing a write-up to brief the executive committee on the grant, and sending out the grant contract once the committee approved it. Nowhere in the process was there a place for outcomes to be negotiated, set, or incorporated. The process would have to be redesigned to include these new steps. Immediately, it became apparent that there was not just one process owner—in fact, all of the program officers were process owners, since each ran the process for their own set of grants. Therefore, in order to make the process work, all would need to be onboard with the new approach. Moreover, training would be necessary, as not all of the program staff were familiar with outcomes measurement. This would take time. Last, different technologies would have to be integrated so that systems could "talk to each other" and exchange data. All this had to be incorporated into the plan.

3. **Rollout.** After considering the issues and deciding to proceed, the benchmarking team planned out the implementation, determining that the entire process would take twelve months to integrate. A fallback plan (in the form of a scaled-down pilot project with only a few program officers) was created in order to begin the implementation sooner. Because training staff on new technology was just as difficult as training them on new evaluation techniques, the benchmarking team decided to do one training at a time. A full-time evaluator was hired on staff to track program officers on outcomes measurement and update their write-ups to include new information. No new technology would be introduced until after

SAMPLE (continued)

six months, when the staff were fluent in the new process and ready to use a technology tool instead of preparing the grant write-ups on paper. A monitoring system was put in place to track feedback on the new system and the board's satisfaction with the enhanced grant reporting. In the meantime, the grants manager worked with the existing software provider and the new technology provider to identify data points and functionality where the systems would integrate.

Process Redesign Schematic

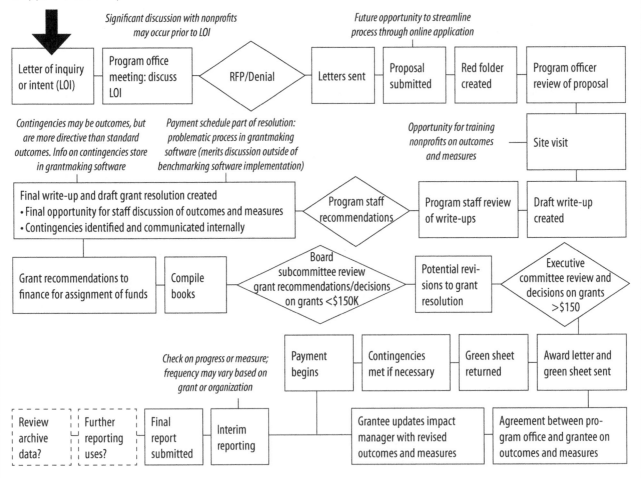

Worksheet 14: Best Practice Implementation Plan

CTQ Outcome Name: _____

I. Internal Goals

Process: _____

Process Owner: _____

Performance Measure: _____

    Baseline: _____

    New Benchmark: _____

Name of Best Practice: _____

Best Practice Contact Info: _____

_____

II. Process Redesign

A. Current Process Schematic:

B. New Process Schematic:

C. Anticipated Implementation Issues:

(continued)

Worksheet 14 continued

III. Rollout

A. Action Steps to Address Implementation Issues:

B. Time Frame:

Start Date: _____, 20_____

1st Checkpoint: _____, 20_____

2nd Checkpoint: _____, 20_____

Full Implementation Date: _____, 20_____

C. Additional Resources or Changes Necessary to Implement:

D. Contingency Plan:

Step 5B: Overcome Staff Resistance

Implementing new processes involves changing human behavior and, in particular, the bane of human behavior—habit. The benchmarking team must be careful to anticipate, identify, and proactively address human concerns within the organization before new ideas are introduced. The benchmarking team will need to communicate the benefits, vision, and mandate for change early and often. The team will also have to work closely with the senior leadership (board, executive director, senior management), line management (program staff, process owners), and other key stakeholders (funders, volunteers, administrative staff). Buy-in is critical.

For some organizations, implementing new ideas will be a no-brainer: the organization is already motivated to do so, has that kind of culture, or is small enough that the benchmarking team itself represents most of the major process owners. For other organizations, benchmarking can be scary and intimidating. It reprioritizes staff routines, creates uncertainty, and elevates what's expected of staff. You should anticipate encountering staff resistance the first time you attempt to implement the results of a benchmarking initiative; if you don't, no worries; if you do, at least you'll be prepared to handle it.

In the example of the community foundation (see Creating an Implementation Plan, page 77), a few of the program officers were totally against the new evaluation initiative. They didn't understand its purpose, didn't know how it benefited them, and didn't want to change the process they were using. What turned them around was the benchmarking champion. In this case, the head of programs sat down with each program officer and explained why the initiative was important to the organization, how it mattered to the board, and how it stood to benefit them in terms of time savings and a new compensation structure. In addition, she made sure that the program officers were invited to help in the process redesign. All of these interventions had the same effect: helping staff understand the problem and making them feel a part of the solution.

> **TIP: Focus on implementation**
>
> The ultimate pitfall in any benchmarking undertaking is to produce a gleaming, impressive benchmarking report, and then have the recommendations go nowhere. The key to success is in the implementation phase. Involve beneficiaries of the process early and often. Hardwire them into the process by having them design the questionnaires, suggest partners, and review your conclusions.

Step 5C: Create a Staff Communication Plan

A well-designed communication plan can go a long way to helping your organization secure support for benchmarking and overcome any potential resistance or fear. Here's a list of the most frequently asked questions you can expect to hear from staff regarding benchmarking:[18]

1. What is it?
   - What is benchmarking all about?
   - Isn't this a manufacturing initiative? How does it relate to our organization and processes?
   - We've been through evaluation, capacity building, and other programs. Is this just another "flavor of the month"?
   - Some of the terminology seems strange. What is the difference between a benchmark, a best practice, and an outcome?

2. What's in it for me?
   - How will this initiative affect me?
   - How will it impact my department?
   - Is this a potential threat or eventual benefit relative to job security?
   - Will there be a role to play even if we're not statisticians?
   - We're already stretched thin—where will we find the time for this?
   - Are there career advantages to participating in benchmarking?

3. What does benchmarking mean for our organization?
   - How will this benefit our constituents or funders?
   - How will managers respond to benchmarking? What role will they play?
   - What are the initial areas targeted for improvement and how soon will we see results?
   - What criteria will be used for selecting best practices and projects?

✔ **TASK:** *Create a Benchmarking Communication Plan*

Take time to complete Worksheet 15: Benchmarking Communication Plan, page 83. It will help you think about all the aspects of informing your organization regarding benchmarking.

---

[18] Adapted from Carolyn Pexton, "Communication Strategies for Six Sigma Initiatives," 2000 (www.isixsigma.com/library/content/c030929a.asp).

Worksheet 15: Benchmarking Communication Plan

Answer the following questions to get you started on formulating a benchmarking communication plan.

1. Who (What target audiences will we need to communicate to?)

2. Self-interests (What are the key interests of each audience that the message needs to satisfy?)

3. What (Do we need to say about our benchmarking initiative, mission, and strategy?)

4. When (How often do we intend to communicate?)

5. Where (How will we reach our audience—what media/venues will we use?)

6. Why (What do we hope to accomplish through this communication strategy?)

7. How (What tone will we use; how do we intend to engage each audience, balancing their self-interests with what we need to communicate?)

Step 5D: Implement the Best Practice

There is little to say about implementation except just do it—and expect it to be challenging and rewarding! Don't be discouraged by failures and complaints, and keep hammering at the communications necessary to help staff feel comfortable. A few tips gleaned from experienced benchmarkers may help in your final rollout:

- Make sure the organization knows its top brass are 100 percent behind this.
- Get a mandate from the board.
- Incorporate benchmarks into your organization's strategic plan.
- Sell the benefits of benchmarking to staff.
- If staff need to be let go because they stand in the way of change, do it immediately.
- Reward employees with compensation to improve performance.
- Prioritize recommendations—don't take on everything at once.
- Communicate positive results quickly.
- Celebrate your success.

Summary

Implementing the best practice you discovered in Chapter 4 is more difficult than just copying a new process. You must consider your organization's resources, structures, and culture. A formal implementation plan will include your reset benchmarks, how your process will be redesigned, what changes need to be made, and a rollout plan.

Making changes in the way your organization works will often create staff resistance. The benchmarking team must proactively address staff concerns before new ideas are implemented. Clear communication is key, and a well-designed communication plan—one that includes information about benchmarking and how it will benefit staff and the organization—goes a long way to ease staff fears.

After all of the preparation, the research, and the analysis, benchmarking comes down to jumping in and making a change. When you see the quality of your organization's work improve, celebrate. Your staff will see the benefit of benchmarking and will implement it in other aspects of their work.

Today's Benchmark Is Tomorrow's Baseline

You cannot strive for excellence once. You need to *continue* to strive to do better. Build benchmarking into your organization's culture so that it occurs almost reflexively. Making this commitment for the long haul improves morale, performance, and outlook, but it requires a constant, vigilant scouting for new ideas and upgrading of old ones.

Today's success should simply be tomorrow's norm. Innovation can be linear (raising the bar on performance) or geometric (creating an entirely new category of performance you never before thought possible). As the world continues to spin forward, the nonprofit sector needs to continue to elevate its game. Nonprofits need to constantly seek out better ways of delivering services, better ways of engaging the communities they serve, more efficient ways of running operations, and more effective means of managing their enterprises.

And remember, benchmarking is itself a process—something that can be measured and *improved*. Indeed many organizations even benchmark *how to benchmark*!

APPENDIX A

Common Outcomes and Performance Measures

While every organization must select the outcomes and measures that are most appropriate for its work, some commonalities are beginning to emerge. Common indicators for financial sustainability, management effectiveness, and community engagement are easier to come by. For example, a quick scan of commonly used financial indicators suggests measuring the diversification of revenue sources, percent of earned income, donor renewals, revenue growth, and positive operating income. Common indicators used to gauge management effectiveness include board meeting attendance, employee turnover rates, percentage of board members as donors, employee satisfaction rates, and technology competency ratings.

The real challenge has been in trying to standardize program metrics. The argument is that every program is different, so how can it be possible to use any common measures? While it is indeed true that each program engages in a different set of activities (that is, every organization has a distinct theory of change), the answer to the puzzle lies in looking at the sector through a different lens. Rather than looking at the sector vertically, that is, by program type, nonprofits must look at the sector horizontally, across programs, to identify and highlight common outcomes.

Irrespective of program type or theory of intervention, many organizations are striving for similar outcomes. Attaching measures to these common "meta-outcomes," rather than common programs, opens up the possibility of cross-comparison and learning. These meta-outcomes typically include changes in knowledge, attitudes, behavior, and status or condition, and assessment of various quality-of-service characteristics. For example, at first glance, a job training program and an arts education program suggest totally different outcomes and measures. Upon closer examination, however, it can be determined that both programs share a common outcome: "improving a skill" (one in the arts, the other in basic job readiness). And there are commonly accepted performance measures to track skill development (for example, pre- and post-test scores, cost per person trained, graduation rates, matriculation rates).

The Woods Fund

Recently the Woods Fund of Chicago, a family foundation led by Ricardo Millett, conducted a learning experiment with a cohort of grantees engaged in different programmatic activities (for example, advocacy, education, and housing). Each organization was asked to complete a logic model. Not surprisingly, each organization's activities and goals were articulated differently. Then, the groups were invited to a "peer-learning" session that focused on sharing common, "horizontal" outcomes rather than "vertical" program activities. What Woods found was incredibly revealing—all organizations were actually pursuing the same set of common outcomes:

- Increased visibility/awareness re: issue X
- Effecting policy change re: issue X
- Engaging constituents and beneficiaries and participation re: issue X
- Increased resources for issue X
- Educated constituents re: issue X
- Improved condition/quality of life in community X
- Influencing stakeholders (of X process)

Here is a list of common outcomes and measures that you can use as a guideline in selecting your own.

Outcome	Associated Impact Area	Associated Measures	Measure Type
Improve Skills	Program	Graduation rate	percent
		People trained	number
		Dropout rate	percent
		Improved skills: level 1–10 (exit survey)	number
		Improved skills: overall (exit survey)	percent
		Placement rate	percent
		Increase in test scores (pre/post)	percent
		Participants report increase in knowledge/skill	percent
		Participants report positive effects or opportunities as a result of knowledge/skills acquired	number
		Recidivism rate	percent
Change Behavior/ Attitude	Program	Participants per course/session/workshop	number
		Participants graduating course/session/workshop	percent
		Participants reporting change in behavior or cessation of activity	percent
		Participants reporting no relapse 6 months after completion/graduation	percent
		Participants reporting no relapse 12 months after completion/graduation	percent
		Participants reporting increased opportunities as a result of behavior change	percent
		Recidivism rate	percent
Reduce Incidence of an Undesirable Activity/ Behavior	Program	Change in rate	percent
		Participants	number
		Community perception of degree of change 1–10 (survey)	number
		Expert rating of change in rate 1–10 (survey)	number
Improve Access to Services	Program	Reported number of community agencies that witness an increase in new participants who came to their agency as a result of a call to the information and referral hotline	number
		Calls to hotline	number
		Increase in calls to hotline	percent
		Participants reporting services were affordable	percent
		Participants who could afford services who couldn't before	percent
		Participants reporting services were useful	percent
		Successful completion of sessions	percent
Improve Conditions (Environmental)	Program	Environmental conditions improved as reported by a trained observer	percent
		Range of improvement 1–10 (trained observer)	number
		Range of improvement 1–10 (participant)	number
		Increase in activity formerly prohibited as a result of past condition having been ameliorated	percent

Outcome	Associated Impact Area	Associated Measures	Measure Type
Improve Awareness	Program	Participants graduating course/session/workshop	percent
		Participants reporting greater awareness of cause/issue	percent
Improve Attendance	Program	Participation rate	percent
		Active participation	percent
Provide Counseling/Advice	Program	Participants	number
		Participants who follow advice or recommended course of action	percent
Improve Quality of Product/Service	Program	Quality rating 1–10 (participants)	number
		Quality rating 1–10 (independent)	number
		Critical reviews	number
		Accreditations/Certifications obtained	number
Create Jobs	Program	Placement rate	percent
		Total jobs created	number
		Length of time (job held)	number
		Offers per attendee	number
		Average salary	dollars
Customer Satisfaction	Program	Customer satisfaction rate	percent
		Level of satisfaction 1–10	number
		Response time	number
		Recommend to others	percent
Improve Efficiency	Program	Cost per person served	dollars
		Unit cost	dollars
		Quality increase	percent
Improve Earned Income	Financial	Total earned income revenue	dollars
		Total net earned income	dollars
		Recurring earned income	percent
		Growth in earned income (annual)	percent
Diversify Income	Financial	Total dollars from grants	percent
		Total dollars from government	percent
		Total earned income	percent
		Total contributed income (donors)	percent
Improve Net Income	Financial	Total net income (annual)	dollars
Adequate Working Capital	Financial	Cash reserves (# of months)	dollars
		Working capital positive	Yes/No

Outcome	Associated Impact Area	Associated Measures	Measure Type
Improve Donor Sustainability	Financial	Foundation grants	number
		Multi-year grants (foundation)	number
		Multi-year grants (government)	number
		Multi-year contracts	number
		New foundation grants	number
		New donors	number
		Revenue per donor	dollars
		Donor retention	percent
		Revenue per retained donor	dollars
		Revenue per new donor	dollars
		Board members as donors	percent
		Frequency of reporting to donors/foundation (times per year)	number
		Quality of reporting 1–10 (board survey)	number
		Quality of reporting 1–10 (donor/foundation survey)	number
Community Engagement	Management	Articles/Press coverage	number
		Site traffic (unique visitors)	number
		Site traffic (return visitors)	number
		Growth in site traffic	percent
		Calls/Inquiries	number
		Volunteers	number
		Growth in calls/inquiries	percent
Board Engagement	Management	Board members as donors	percent
		Board attendance	percent
		Board meeting frequency (times per year)	number
Accountability	Management	Board-approved strategic plan	Yes/No
		Full-time CEO	Yes/No
		Board-approved technology plan	Yes/No
		D&O insurance	Yes/No
		CEO succession plan	Yes/No
Employee Satisfaction	Management	Turnover rate	percent
		Performance reviews (average for all employees on 1–10 scale)	number
Technology	Management	Fund accounting system	Yes/No
		Donor database	Yes/No
		Software licensing compliance	percent
		Cost per employee	dollars
		Performance measurement system	Yes/No

Benchmarking Software Selection Criteria

As more organizations begin to benchmark and measure performance, new tools are being created to automate the process. Similar to the way accounting software has been developed to help many different organizations measure and track financial performance, benchmarking tools have been developed to help different organizations measure and track nonfinancial measures.

Depending on the scope and complexity of your benchmarking efforts, your organization may want to explore software solutions to document your learning. Microsoft Excel and other basic spreadsheets are sufficient to handle basic data collection. For more advanced benchmarking, specialized tools are available to help nonprofit organizations keep track of many different indicators over time, reporting on progress toward benchmark levels of performance. When searching for the right tool, keep these criteria in mind:

1. Avoid outcome-only tools

- Limited to human services agencies
- Only work for tracking programmatic outcomes
- Case-management dependent

2. Look for robust applications, not just technology

- Search for software programs designed for this purpose
- Avoid custom databases
- Select programs that offer product upgrades, add-on services

3. Look for ease of use and flexibility

- Must be able to measure the processes you have now and might have in the future

- Reporting must be flexible but not open-ended

4. Bet on subject-matter expertise

- What is the company's core competency?

- Does the product have vision or is it one-dimensional?

- What do thought leaders think of the company/leadership?

Bibliography

Ammons, David N. *Municipal Benchmarks: Assessing Local Performance and Establishing Community Standards.* 2d ed. Thousand Oaks, CA: Sage Publications, 2001.

Bok, Derek. *The State of the Nation.* Cambridge, MA: Harvard University Press, 1996.

Camp, Robert C. *Benchmarking: The Search for Industry Best Practices That Lead to Superior Performance.* Milwaukee, WI: ASQC Quality Press, 1989.

de Bono, Edward. *Lateral Thinking: Creativity Step by Step.* New York: Perennial Library, 1990.

Drucker, Peter F. *The Drucker Foundation Self-Assessment Tool Participant Workbook.* San Francisco: Jossey-Bass Publishers, 1999.

———. *Managing the Non-Profit Organization: Principles and Practices.* New York: HarperBusiness, 1992.

Gore, Al. *Common Sense Government: Works Better and Costs Less.* New York: Random House, 1995.

Grossman, Allen, and Arthur McCaffrey. "Jumpstart." *Harvard Business School Case Study 9-301-037,* 2001.

Harrington, H. James. *High Performance Benchmarking: 20 Steps to Success.* New York: McGraw-Hill, 1996.

Harvard Business School. *Harvard Business Review on Nonprofits.* Cambridge, MA: Harvard Business School Press, 1999.

Hodgkinson, Virginia A., and Richard W. Lyman and Associates. *The Future of the Nonprofit Sector.* San Francisco: Jossey-Bass, 1989.

Keehley, Patricia, Steven Medlin, Sue MacBride, and Laura Longmire. *Benchmarking for Best Practices in the Public Sector: Achieving Performance Breakthroughs in Federal, State, and Local Agencies.* San Francisco: Jossey-Bass, 1997.

Knauft, E.B., Renee A. Berger, and Sandra T. Gray. *Profiles of Excellence: Achieving Success in the Nonprofit Sector.* San Francisco: Jossey-Bass, 1991.

Letts, Christine W., William P. Ryan, and Allen Grossman. *High Performance Nonprofit Organizations: Managing Upstream for Greater Impact.* New York: John Wiley & Sons, 1999.

Newcomer, Kathryn K. *Using Performance Measurement to Improve Public and Nonprofit Programs.* San Francisco: Jossey-Bass, no. 75, Fall 1997.

Osborne, David, and Ted Gaebler. *Reinventing Government: How the Entrepreneurial Spirit Is Transforming the Public Sector.* New York: Penguin Group, 1993.

Peters, Thomas J. *In Search of Excellence: Lessons from America's Best-Run Companies.* New York: Harper & Row, 1982.

Sawhill, John, and David Williamson. "Measuring What Matters in Nonprofits." *The McKinsey Quarterly,* no. 2 (2001): 98–107.

Watson, Gregory H. *The Benchmarking Workbook: Adapting Best Practices for Performance Improvement.* Portland, OR: Productivity Press, 1992.